Captive of Culture

**Culture and Its Relevance
in a Religious Community**

Captive of Culture

Culture and Its Relevance in a Religious Community

Roy Chicago
Chicago, Illinois

Tercentenary Publication
2010

Captive of Culture: Culture and Its Relevance in a Religious Community – published by the Rev. Dr. Ashish Amos of the Indian Society for Promoting Christian Knowledge (ISPCK), Post Box 1585, 1654, Madarsa Road, Kashmere Gate, Delhi-110006.

© Author, 2010

All rights reserved. No part of this book may be reproduced or transmitted in any form or by any means, electronic, mechanical, photocopying, recording, or by any information storage and retrieval system, without the prior permission in writing from the publisher.

The views expressed in the book are those of the author and the publisher takes no responsibility for any of the statements.

ISBN: 978-81-8465-072-3

Cover Design : V.C. John

Laser typeset by
ISPCK, Post Box 1585, 1654, Madarsa Road, Kashmere Gate, Delhi-110006 • *Tel:* 23866323

e-mail: ashish@ispck.org.in • ella@ispck.org.in
website: www.ispck.org.in

contents

Foreword .... *vii*
Preface .... *ix*
Prologue .... *xiii*
Acknowledgements .... *xv*
Introduction .... *xvii*

Chapter - 1
Culture and Faith   **1-12**

1.1. Culture   1
1.2. Faith   8

Chapter - 2
Culture: Its Relation to Faith, Religion, Christ,
Bible, Society, Mission and Ministry   **14-49**

2.1. Culture and Faith   14
2.2. Culture and Religion   17
2.3. Culture and Christ   21
2.4. Culture and Bible   27
2.5. Culture and Society   31
2.6. Culture and Mission   39
2.7. Culture and Ministry   45

Chapter - 3

**Culture and Immigrants, Islamic Culture in
North America and Culture and Communities**   50-71

3.1. Culture and Immigrants   50

3.2. Islamic Culture in North America   56

3.3. Culture and Communities   64

Chapter - 4

Indian Culture and Christianity in India   72-81

4.1. Indian Culture   72

4.2. Christianity in India   77

Chapter - 5

**Church of South India (CSI) and Church of
South India in North America**   82-96

5.1. Church of South India (CSI)   82

5.2. Church of South India in North America   88

CONCLUSION   97-100

BIBLIOGRAPHY   101-104

Foreword

In an increasingly diverse world how are Christians to understand the complex relationships between culture and faith? Multiculturalism is a fact of life in the cities, suburbs and towns of western society and more and more throughout the world. Communication technologies and the relative ease of travel bring us daily face to face with cultural contexts not our own. Patterns of immigration and economic necessity mean that our immediate neighbors may well be persons of entirely different backgrounds, customs, expectations and worldviews. The Christian faith has been planted throughout the world and taken root in the soil of many different cultures and peoples. The faith itself may be recognizably the same, but it appears in the dress of quite distinctive cultures. When those cultures encounter one another and even move next door to one another, how does the cultural clothing impact the faith that promises to make believers in Christ one Body?

Mathew Idicula deftly explores answers to these questions through multiple lenses. First, he examines the broad implications of faith in Christ as it takes form necessarily in terms of particular cultural contexts. Beginning with Niebuhr's classic categories of Christ and culture he leads us to consider how the earliest Christian community's experience of faith grew and developed as it moved out into the cultures of its original missionary contexts. He lays before us the ongoing challenges of that encounter, from culturally conditioned expectations about the role of women to sexuality to social customs. Finally, he focuses his attention on the missional implications of all this for the particular life and health of the churches of India as they live now in the context of North American culture.

Father Mathew's recurring theme is that however the cultural contexts may change, the church's life is founded not on them, but rather on the life, death and resurrection of Jesus Christ. In the emerging culture of a post-modern world, no theme could be more important for Christian believers. Will the diversity of human culture be embraced as a sign of God's generous creativity or will it be a source of division and increasing rancor? For Christians who live out their faith as members of churches bearing an Indian heritage as well as those in their partner churches, it is good to be reminded that our common identity finally transcends all cultural contexts. There is one Lord, one faith, one baptism, one God and Father of all. Mathew Idicula proclaims that truth with clarity and conviction.

Rt. Rev. Jeffrey D. Lee
Bishop of the Epicopal/Anglican Diocese of Chicago

Preface

This book represents an effort on my part to share with you my reflections concerning the dominant role of culture and its embodiment, seen in a host of religious dimensions. These reflections and convictions are mine. They are deeply held because they are born out of my experiences of more than half a century in two dominant cultures. I offer my personal experiences, which have come from my own cultural traditions and experiences as a child in India and as an adult in North America. This book also reflects the challenges of understanding culture as a powerful reality shaping faith and life. It shares my personal values as one of the leaders of the Church of South India community in North America. This book also shows my vocation as an Anglican priest called to build a multicultural congregation in suburban Chicago.

I came to the United States in 1972 as a young adult to enhance my educational qualifications. It did not take me long to recognize the difficulty in reclaiming my former home in India. My life during the last four decades seeking a prosperous future and hoping to participate in this new land was not an easy journey. I faced the challenges of finding employment, securing a place to live, and gaining confidence in using the

English language as spoken and understood by Americans. In my early years of life in my adopted culture, I often faced many problems, including racial discrimination. Often, I wondered how I would find a faith community and house of worship where I could be further nurtured in my acquired Christian faith brought with me from South India. Those early years in Chicago were difficult and often confusing. From the very beginning, I was in the forefront as a leader forming a faith community suitable for my fellow Church of South India Christians and their future generations.

From my teenage years, I was very aware that God was calling me to become a priest. My ordination would necessitate more years of waiting. My theological studies were completed in the Lutheran School of Theology at Chicago. As an ordained priest, I quickly realized that my engagement with cultural issues and their religious significance would now become a major concern of my ministry. Wherever I have labored for the sake of the Gospel, I am continually amazed to see how important people's cultural background is to them, as it relates to the congregation. This includes their ways of worship, parish fellowship, family values, and ethnic traditions.

This book seeks to enumerate many areas where I have witnessed the powerful impact and influence of local culture and inherited ethnic values on Christian worship practices and congregational life.

In several sections of this book, I have quoted from the perspectives, positions, definitions, and conclusions of numerous cultural scholars whose written work is well regarded in the academic field. However, I am not convinced that any one scholar has been able to be sufficiently inclusive, or has demonstrated the depth and breadth of culture, or has adequately expressed the passion and loyalty that culture evokes in the actual experience of people who have shared life, worship, faith, values, and fellowship with me! Therefore, I now invite the reader to give attention to my personal journey, my cultural viewpoints, and strong convictions, which have been nurtured, developed, challenged, and pragmatically applied, to the mission and practice of Christian leadership and ministry in North America.

Prologue

The book 'Captive of Culture' by Rev. Dr. Mathew Idicula is a scholarly assessment of Christians migrated to USA from the background of the Church of South India. They have distinct cultural and religious identity. In fact, as he himself has expressed, this book is a product of his own experience, struggles and knowledge about the CSI people living in USA.

Considerable numbers of people are living in the United State from the background of the Church of South India. They are made to participate in two different cultural settings. He has rightly pointed out that every one is integrally related to ones own culture. They inherited the culture of the people of India as well as the culture of the migrate land. In most cases the motive behind migration has been economic security and employment opportunities. The expression of their faith is unique and therefore they keep their identity as a community of "God's people" in an alien land and culture. He makes an indirect plea to the leadership of the Church that culturally oriented structural and administrative frame work be formed for the immigrant people in USA from the Church of South India.

The author has made elaborate study on the culture and faith of the people in general and the immigrants in USA. This study is on the one hand based on the teachings of the Bible and on the other his assessment of the Indian and U S Societies. The plurality of the people and the culture, makes it all the more important that the culture which has been adopted should be given due consideration. The author also compares the life of the CSI Christians with that of some other cultural or ethnic groups of Christians in USA from South India. This book is informative and at the same time an asset to the ministry to the people from different cultures living in America. This also will help the ministerial organization for people living in other traditions and cultures.

My congratulations to Rev. Dr. Mathew Idicula for bringing out this volume. I also wish God's blessings to all the readers of this book.

The Most Rev.Dr.J.W.Gladtone
Moderator (Former) & Bishop of the Church of South India

Acknowledgements

First of all, let me thank God Almighty for giving me an opportunity to publish this book. I was born in India, a culture almost entirely different from the West. At the time of my birth there was no electricity in our village. **I have been living most of my life in the United States of America, a country very different from the place where I was born and spent my childhood days.**

Life was never easy for me even though I was very fortunate to have so many opportunities in my life. Always, I had to overcome challenges and difficulties. However, the more I am challenged the more I become determined to complete my goals. From early on, church, Sunday school, and prayer were some of the priorities of my life. I started theological studies out of curiosity to grow more deeply into theology. The more I studied, the more I was challenged to learn about Christianity and the Christian religion. Seminary was like an extended family to me. The last ten years that I spent in the seminary were indeed a memorable time of my life. I found many new friends and got to know many good people. During the course of my studies, I did not always agree with what I was learning. I had my own beliefs on many issues. Seminary did not change my faith or beliefs, only my theological knowledge and understanding. **I never thought that I will be achieving this great accomplishment especially at this stage of my life. This book is about my experiences on both sides of the globe.**

There are many people I am indebted to as I completed my studies. In addition to my family, I want to thank all my professors and advisors who taught me many valuable lessons and all those who made my theological studies a reality. I want to dedicate this book to my eldest son, Mathew P. Idicula Jr., who was very instrumental in my theological studies. **Once again, I thank and praise God Almighty who guides me through the green pastures and leads me in the right path.** "The Lord is my shepherd, I shall not want" (Psalm 23:1, NRSV).

Roy Chicago

Introduction

God made us in His own image. "Let us make humankind in our image, according to our likeness; and let them have dominion over the fish of the sea, and the birds of the air, and over the cattle, and over all the wild animals of the earth, and over every creeping thing that that creeps upon the earth" (Genesis 1:26, NRSV). Our physical bodies are different, but we all reflect God's glory. Our looks and behavior are different, but we all have the ability to reflect God's character in our love, patience, forgiveness, kindness, and faithfulness. "By contrast, the fruit of the Spirit is love, joy, peace, patience, kindness, generosity, faithfulness, gentleness, and self-control" (Galatians 5:22-23, NRSV). People living on this planet also differ in their language, lifestyle, and culture depending on their location in life. In other words, we are different, not because of our choice, but because of **factors** beyond our control. Food, environment, climate, faith, customs, and manners are all aspects of our difference.

Through this book, I will briefly analyze the importance of culture in religious fellowship, particularly in the Church of South India (CSI) community in North America. During the early part of the 1970s, South Indian Christians migrated to

North America for economic opportunities. For the first immigrant community their priority was **mainly** their economic satisfaction. As the community grew, they became aware of their cultural and religious needs. **In order to address these longings, they imported their faith community from their own culture and background.** This work will examine the complex relationship between culture and religion in the life of an immigrant church community in the U.S., while paying particular attention to the **fellowship, and its religious and cultural existence.** To understand the contemporary challenges facing the fellowship in the Church of South India community in the U.S., I will explore the history of the church from its earliest communities and draw critical lessons.

In this book I will also present the positions of different cultural scholars, and offer my understanding of cultural relevance in a worshiping community in the light of my experience with the Church of South India community in North America. My understanding of culture and fellowship is based on my personal experience, since I spent the first two decades of my life in India and the last four in North America. In my personal life I have made many adjustments and embraced many new habits and practices from both cultures.

CHAPTER - 1
Culture and Faith

1.1. Culture

The word culture is often defined as historical experiences. Land, environment, social life, and religion all play a part in the development of culture. Language, food, clothing, life style, art, and music are all important factors influencing our culture. Culture is human experience in life. Culture is the experience of a people over the ages in history. Experience is what is not learned by scientific method; rather, it is guided by human behavior. According to Richard Kroner, "Science has to return to direct experience over and over again to check and to verify its knowledge. Trust in pre-scientific experience is indispensable to the operation of reason."[1] Experience is given to us by our behavior and action. It is not learned by scientific scrutiny but guided by human nature. "Experience may be described as the procedure of becoming directly, i.e., by an immediate contact, acquainted with the object of knowledge."[2]

Experience is not always a sure method of acquiring knowledge, but it is the principle source of knowledge.

---

[1] Richard Kroner, *Culture and Faith* (Chicago: The University of Chicago Press, 1951), 18.
[2] *Ibid.*, 13.

"What we experience is in some way given to us; we do not produce it. Experience is accompanied by the consciousness of certainty, although this certainty may be questioned either by new experiences or by reason."[3] Life in this world produces experience and we cannot live without experience. Human experience is different from scientific experience. "Scientific experience is impersonal in a twofold sense: it is neither an experience of persons, personal relations, personal institutions, and so forth, nor an experience of personal relevancy and significance."[4] But human experiences produce civilizations and cultures. Fellowship of people over a period of time produces human experiences, and human experience produces culture. In his book, *Culture and Faith,* Kroner describes culture as the life experience of people over a period of time.

This world is different in many ways. Culture develops out of our difference. It informs aspects of our behavior determining our perceptions, our way of thinking, our faith, and our religious experience. "A cultural system is therefore a configuration of symbols that acts as a bridge between ideas and behavior. Religion itself is such a cultural system."[5] Our experiences of life differ according to our pattern of living. Culture not only shapes our behavior but also shapes our ideas. "Culture is therefore essentially a transmitted pattern of meanings embodied in symbols, a pattern capable of development and change, and it belongs to the concept of humanness itself."[6]

---

[3] *Ibid.*
[4] *Ibid.,* 20.
[5] Aylward Shorter, *Toward a Theology of Inculturation* (London: Biddles Ltd, 1988), 40.
[6] *Ibid.,* 5.

Experience and culture are not different but blended.

> Experience and culture or civilization are not two different modes of human life, they are intrinsically interwoven as stages in a development. Culture is an outcome of experience, and experience issues in cultural activity, in man's self-civilizing exertions and performances.[7]

Culture comes from human experience, and human experience develops civilization. "Experience motivates cultural activity, it contains the task or sets the purpose which is carried through in the multiplicity of activities unfolded in civilization."[8] Culture is the work of human effort. Land, language, and social life play a part in the development of culture. H. Richard Niebuhr describes culture thus:

> Culture is the work of men's minds and hands. It is that portion of man's heritage in any place or time which has been given us designedly and laboriously by other men, not what has come to us via the mediation of nonhuman beings or through human beings insofar as they have acted without intention of results or without control of the process. Hence it includes speech, education, tradition, myth, science, art, philosophy, government, law, rite, beliefs, inventions, technologies.[9]

Culture is what the human being learns and experiences as a member of society. Human beings not only produce culture, but also distinguish one another in terms of culture. More often human society is identified also in terms of its culture:

> The more modern tendency is to reverse the order and to define human society in terms of culture. According to this way of thinking, it is what human beings share culturally, their customs, values and distinctive way of living that constitutes them as a recognizably distinct human group

---

[7] Kroner, *Culture and Faith*, 22.

[8] *Ibid.*, 22.

[9] H. Richard Niebuhr, *Christ and Culture* (New York: Harper & Row Publishers, 1975), 33.

or society. Human societies not only possess a culture, but are distinguished by it from other human societies. [10]

Culture has a broader meaning. "It connotes the entire mental setup acquired through the geographical, ethnic, linguistic, familial, professional, social and religious environment, covering among other fields food and cuisine, forms of work and recreation, ways of dressing, daily and yearly rhythms of life, type of imagination, symbolic fields, and so on."[11] Human beings interact with one another according to their preconceived mental patterns, "Culture is therefore not simply about behaviour. It is also about ideas."[12]

Culture is not limited to time or place. Culture changes the world, the patterns, the behavior, social customs, and civilizations. Culture itself is the product of change. Culture changes from time to time and from place to place. The culture of one place may not be the culture of another place. The culture of one time may not be the culture of another time. According to Aylward Shorter, "All cultures, therefore, throughout history have undergone a form of regular change in which the structures of society and its patterns of thought have remained intact."[13] Culture differs from society to society, community to community, race to race, and **religion to religion**. The culture of one society, community, race, or religion may not be the culture of another. Culture has an influence in every level of human life. Culture also changes according to people's customs, manners, and scientific advancement. Culture is not something **we inherit or given to us** by another; rather, it is something constantly changing as a result of our habits and surrounding.

---

[10] Shorter, *Toward a Theology of Inculturation*, 4.
[11] Lucien Legrand, *The Bible on Culture* (Maryknoll, New York: Orbis Books, 2000), 73-74.
[12] Shorter, *Toward a Theology of Inculturation*, 4.
[13] Shorter, *Toward a Theology of Inculturation*, 45.

Culture is not handed to us; rather, we construct it by picking and choosing items "from the shelves of the past and the present" (Nagel 1994, 162). As a result, cultures are in a constant state of dynamic flux; they are borrowed, blended, rediscovered, and reinterpreted.[14]

Throughout the centuries, culture has played an important role in faith and formation of religious beliefs. For this reason, the culture of a society always will reflect the religious community of that society. "American Christianity in the first two decades of the twentieth century was directly impacted, of course, by more than scientific discoveries and technological inventions as such."[15]

During the last two decades Christianity, especially Western Christianity, has readjusted itself according to the changes in the community.

Our culture is also an important part of our religious beliefs. People having the same values gathering together for religious fellowship and religious worship form a common culture. This is called inculturation. **"A short definition of inculturation is: the on-going dialogue between faith and culture or cultures. More fully, it is the creative and dynamic relationship between the Christian message and a culture or cultures."**[16] Inculturation happens when the **religious message transforms culture** and is itself transformed by culture. "Inculturation implies that the Christian message transforms a culture. It is also the case that Christianity is transformed by culture, not in

---

[14] Shoshanah Feher, "From the Rivers of Babylon to the Valleys of Los Angeles: The Exodus and Adaptation of Iranian Jews" *Gatherings in Diaspora: Religious Communities and the New Immigration*. Edited by R. Stephen Warner and Judith G. Wittner (Philadelphia: Temple University Press, 1998), 80.

[15] Phyllis Tickle, *The Great Emergence: How Christianity is Changing and Why* (Grand Rapids, Michigan: Baker Books, 2008), 87.

[16] *Ibid.*, 11.

a way that falsifies the message."[17] Christian fellowship is the gathering of people sharing the same Christian values. These people have common goals and common values. They have a common belief and a common culture. They are united in their language, dress code, understanding of their faith beliefs, and often they have the same problems to share with each other.

After the resurrection of Jesus Christ, the disciples returned to Jerusalem and secluded themselves for several days of fasting and prayer. "All these were constantly devoting themselves to prayer, together with certain women, including Mary the mother of Jesus, as well as his brothers" (Acts 1:14, NRSV). That was the beginning of Christian history and churches in the first century. The main goal of the early church was to survive, so they came together in fellowship with a common goal and common faith. Fellowship was an important part of them coming together. What united the early Christians was the Christian message. Indeed, they had a common fellowship and a common goal. "They devoted themselves to the apostles' teaching and fellowship, to the breaking of bread and the prayers." (Acts 2:42, NRSV). Their culture was very much a part of their beliefs. And, their common faith was in the crucified and risen Jesus Christ. "All who believed were together and had all things in common; they would sell their possessions and goods and distribute the proceeds to all, as any had need" (Acts 2:44-45, NRSV). They believed that Jesus was the answer to their problems in life. In the days of their persecution they met in secret places like underground tombs. They celebrated the Lord's Supper in remembrance of how Jesus had delivered them from sin and expressed their hope for the day when Christ would return. The earliest Christian communities had the most significant impact on Christian churches. Until the fourth century, persecution was severe, and

---

[17] Shorter, *Toward a Theology of Inculturation*, 14.

people were faithful to the cause of Jesus. They saw no need to form a system of church government. But later they realized that they must have a church government in order for them to survive and grow. The pattern of worship established by the early church was informal—praise, meal, preaching, and prayer. They came together for community worship. They also shared their common possessions. "Now the whole group of those who believed were of one heart and soul, and no one claimed private ownership of any possessions, but everything they owned was held in common." (Acts 4:32, NRSV) They witnessed to Jesus in their lives, and they believed in the leadership of Jesus Christ. They came together for fellowship in Jesus' name. They believed that Christ will come in the same way he went into heaven. They waited for that promise and came together with that goal in their lives.

The early Christian community had a culture, a collective culture of Jews and Gentiles. Many of them were from the Jewish faith. Early Christian converts also included Gentiles. Early converts brought along a culture, a culture of their own to the Christian community. In 1 Corinthians, Saint Paul clearly asks people to abandon their immoralities. They could no longer be part of their old habits and practices. "I am writing to you not to associate with anyone who bears the name of brother or sister who is sexually immoral or greedy, or is an idolater, reviler, drunkard, or robber. Do not even eat with such a one" (1Corinthians 5:11, NRSV). The instruction to not even eat with immoral believers presumably included barring them from participating in the Lord's Supper. However, some of them brought their old habits to the Christian faith. The early Christian community had people with pagan cultural habits. Sexual immorality, drinking, greed, idolatry were some of their old habits. From the diversity of their culture, a culture of Jewish community and Gentile community, a common missional culture was formed with a common goal in life. This new culture was the result of their common faith and witness. Thus, inculturation occurred in the early Christian community. "A term that is frequently used in this connection is 'message'. Thus, inculturation is said to be a dialogue between the Christian message and a human culture. We have already seen that this message does not exist independently of culture."[18]

Culture also plays an integral part in all religious expressions including worship. Every religious ritual is culturally formed. The early Christian community had their own ritual culture. They came together to strengthen their fellowship and faith. Their common faith was re-enacted in their fellowship. "The early Christians were not unconcerned with truth or with the scriptural bases for their action. In fact, it is noteworthy that Acts 15:15-18 records that the apostles sought (Old Testament) scriptural justification for the adaptation that they made."[19] Culture and church are very closely integrated throughout history.

1.2. Faith

Faith is the expression of mystical experience, and mystical experience is the foundation of faith. Our faith is the result of our experience beyond this world. "Faith is latent in experience, but experience does not produce faith."[20] Faith is not **an emotion**. "Faith is not a 'feeling' which we either have or have not by instinct."[21] Faith is beyond reality and surpasses all our powers of discovery in this world. "To have faith in someone is to rely upon him and to recognize what he tells us as true

---

[18] *Ibid.*, 59.
[19] Charles H. Kraft, *Christianity in Culture* (Maryknoll, New York: Orbis Books, 1980), 38.
[20] Kroner, *Culture and Faith*, 29.
[21] Eugene Joly, *What is Faith* (New York: Hawthorn Books Publishers, 1960), 16. (check publisher name looks OK to me, more explanation in the bibliography area.)

in virtue of the confidence which we have in him."[22] In Christianity, faith in Jesus Christ surpasses our powers of discovery by witness or scientific methods. "To have faith is to have confidence in God's witnesses, and above all to have confidence in Jesus Christ, and so to stake one's life on Jesus Christ."[23] Faith is the basis of human living and existence. Faith gives human beings hope in life. Indeed, faith sustains hope in human life and human existence. "The faith is about something that happened, something unique and unrepeatable that God did. It is not an idea but history, not a cult but an event."[24] Faith is the response of human beings to God who encounters them. "If we have no faith in the absolute faithfulness of God-in-Christ, it will doubtless be difficult for us to discern the relativity of our faith."[25]

Faith is also the result of our knowledge and education. "It is an act of the intelligence which requires, in order that we may have confidence in Jesus Christ, guarantees that this confidence is deserved. It is also an act of the intelligence which tries to understand the message of Jesus, to grasp its coherence and its value."[26]

Faith is not our experience of the past. It is about our future experience. Faith is our mystical experience about the future. Faith is the trust in mystical experience. "Faith is, in the first place, a certain trust in that ultimate reality which is 'revealed" by the articulation of mystical experience."[27] The basis of our mystical experience evolves from our past experience in life.

---

[22] *Ibid.*, 15-16.
[23] *Ibid.*, 16.
[24] M.M. Thomas, *Society and Religion*, ed. Richard W. Taylor (Madras: Christian Literature Society, 1976), 168.
[25] Niebuhr, *Christ and Culture*, 239.
[26] Joly, *What is Faith*, 16.
[27] Kroner, *Culture and Faith* 195.

We believe in things beyond our capability. Often we realize our powerlessness in this world. Faith gives us hope of things beyond our capability and power. Faith is the belief beyond our control. Faith sustains life in this world. Faith is necessary and inevitable because of the uncertainties in life. "Faith is possible and necessary because man does not now and never will reach the goal of his aspirations, cultural as well as moral."[28] In the midst of uncertainties, faith is the opposite of uncertainties. "We have faith in the account which our perception conveys to us, but this faith is incomplete and fragmentary as long as the account itself is incomplete and fragmentary or while it remains nothing but an account of perception."[29] **Faith is also the result of determination or choice**. "It is also and necessarily an act of the will, for the will is necessary if this inquiry is to be pursued. It is equally indispensable for making our lives follow the direction in which Christ leads us, for life is known only by living it and love only by loving."[30]

All religion is based on faith; it grows out of faith. Faith beliefs are sustained by trust. Religion is a necessary aspect of human life. It is a known fact that even with all the scientific advancements and knowledge, human beings cannot and will not control human destiny. Human beings depend on faith for unanswered questions in their life. "This means that faith is the state of being grasped by an ultimate concern, and God is the name of the content of the concern."[31] Religious faith is an articulation of mystery. "Religious faith loses its original and true meaning when it is deprived of the mystical experience

---

[28] *Ibid.*, 192.
[29] *Ibid.*, 28.
[30] Joly, *What is Faith*, 16.
[31] Paul Tillich, *Theology of Culture* (New York: Oxford University Press, 1959), 40.

out of which it arises and which it interprets or articulates."[32] In 1870, the Vatican Council defined faith as an unmerited favor from God. "Faith is a supernatural virtue, by which, guided and aided by divine grace, we hold as true what God has revealed, not because we have perceived its intrinsic truth by our reason but because of the authority of God who can neither deceive nor be deceived."[33]

Faith, religion, and culture are closely connected. Religious faith contains cultural and moral elements. Faith is belief in hope and meaning while living in the midst of uncertainties. "The presence of faith within life indicates that man is unable to know absolute and total truth about reality, life, and himself by means of reason alone."[34] Even though experience does not produce faith, culture and faith are very much related. Culture forms faith, and faith is expressed in cultural behavior. Faith differs from religion to religion and community to community, as does its expression from culture to cultures. "Religious experience is bound up with cultural development, but nevertheless it has its own character, even at the most highly developed stage of culture."[35]

There have always been tensions between faith, culture, morality, fact, and philosophy. Faith transcends culture and triumphs over it, but culture is also endangered by faith, because tensions always exist between faith and culture. "Because faith transcends the whole cultural horizon and surpasses the very meaning and function of cultural potentialities, the value of culture is endangered."[36] Morality and behavior question faith, so there has always been tension between them. "It is hard to love one's enemy when the enemy

---

[32] Kroner, *Culture and Faith*, 187.
[33] Joly, *What is Faith*, 130.
[34] Kroner, *Culture and Faith*, 191.
[35] *Ibid.*, 30.
[36] *Ibid.*, 239.

is also the enemy of God, and it may even be doubtful whether we are permitted or commanded to love him."[37] There is always tension between fact and faith. If there is no tension between them, faith would not be faith. "The original fall of Adam and Eve as reported in Genesis is certainly not a fact, either of prehistoric or of biological relevance; but it is more relevant to human life than all prehistoric and biological facts can possibly be."[38]

In Christian faith, tension between religion and culture is due to the sinful nature of humanity. This was the general attitude of the early Christian churches.

> For some of them culture is essentially Godless in the purely secular sense, as having neither positive nor negative relation to the God of Jesus Christ; for others it is Godless in the negative sense, as being anti-God or idolatrous; for others it seems solidly based on a natural, rational knowledge of God or His law.[39]

They believed that culture is "Godless in the purely secular sense." One cannot serve two masters, and Christ and culture are identified as two different counterpoints. Fidelity to Jesus necessarily meant the rejection of society. They lived for a life away from the world and looked for a life with God not of the world, but in the world.

> The relation of the authority of Jesus Christ to the authority of culture is such that every Christian must often feel himself claimed by the Lord to reject the world and its kingdoms with their pluralism and temporalism, their makeshift compromises of many interests, their hypnotic obsession by the love of life and the fear of death.[40]

---

[37] *Ibid.*, 247.
[38] *Ibid.*, 249.
[39] Niebuhr, *Christ and Culture*, 30.
[40] *Ibid.*, 68.

Culture and Faith

These tensions and questions will remain as long as faith and religion exist; without it, faith won't be faith. For Christianity, faith is the result of divine guidance, God's grace. Faith is the result of God's revelation in Jesus. It is a reality that our Lord Jesus Christ came to this world to save us from our sin. "We also constantly give thanks to God for this, that when you received the word of God that you heard from us, you accepted it not as a human word but as what it really is, God's word, which is also at work in you believers" (1 Thessalonians 2:13, NRSV).

CHAPTER - 2
Culture: Its Relation to Faith, Religion, Christ, Bible, Society, Mission and Ministry

2.1 Culture and Faith

Culture and faith are closely connected. Culture comes from human experience. "As human experience motivates and produces civilization, so it also contains the rudiments and roots of spiritual faith."[1] Faith is the opposite of doubt. Experience is the result of faith, and experience comes out of faith. Faith comes from hope, and hope is grounded in the promises of God. We live in an uncertain world, and uncertainties create doubt and question faith. In a certain world there is no need for faith, but no such world exists. Faith comes from mystical experience. "Faith is thus suggested by experience, at least with respect to the feeling of mystery which is an inherent and indispensable element of both experience and faith."[2]

---

[1] Kroner, *Culture and Faith*, 27.
[2] *Ibid.*, 28.

Culture

Faith is also the opposite of experience. Experience is certainty of what has happened. Culture is the result of experience. Culture is the product of experience of life over a period of time. "Culture in this deepest sense is an attempt to find the 'giver' of the given, the sender of the message, that we trust."[3] Kroner interprets Schleiermacher, who understands religion as "religion which is itself the product or reflex of culture."[4]

The cultural mind is strangely imprisoned within its own horizon but feels that there is something outside, a light which does not shine within its own compass. Faith alone can provide man with that light, because it must shine in from outside the cultural walls if it is to be genuine and fulfil the task we expect from it.[5]

Scientific knowledge and advancements are products of human culture and civilization. But their role in culture is limited. "The world as propounded by science is by no means the 'world-in-itself' or the whole of experience; it is a limited, definite, fragmentary view of the world, correct within its scope and exact in its knowledge."[6]

All religions are the product of faith. Religion comes out of faith experience. Each culture has its own faith and religious experience. Many of these experiences are also closely connected. "The Indian Mahabharata relates the battle of Kurukshetra between the Pandavas and their close relatives, the Kauravs. Greek literature has dramatized the cruel conflicts between the brothers Orestes, Aigisthos, and Agamamemnon in the house of Atreus."[7]

---

[3] *Ibid.*, 29.
[4] *Ibid.*, 30.
[5] *Ibid.*, 29, 30.
[6] *Ibid.*, 107.
[7] Legrand, *The Bible on Culture*, 16.

Many biblical stories also find parallels in other religions. Religious stories may have some similarities, but differ in the context of each culture. In Christianity, Jesus Christ is the hope of salvation. Christian churches are closely related to the culture of the region. The rituals, organization, customs, and beliefs in Christian churches have changed over the years, but Christian faith remains the same. In Christian culture, God is very much reflected in the culture of the region. Over the years, culture and faith have always been related and remain so. Every religion has its own culture, and religion always has an influence on the culture in which it operates. We can witness this close relationship of culture and religion throughout the centuries.

Christian churches in their rituals and patterns of worship have changed over the years, yet Christian faith endures beyond cultural patterns. Today's growing churches are different from traditional churches in many ways. For example, Willow Creek Community Church in the western suburb of Chicago, and other mega churches all over the country, is following a worship pattern different from that of traditional churches but in keeping with the changing needs and patterns of society. "Willow Creek Community Church has discovered a trend in recent years that led them to another significant innovation in lay ministry."[8] The traditional churches are based on local customs and manners and are there by virtue of the culture of the community, but Christianity is based on the person and teachings of Jesus Christ. Many Christian churches are changing according to the felt needs and demands of the community. "Most traditional churches, despite the loyalty and devotion of their people and the conscientiousness of their

---

[8] George Hunter III, *Church for the Unchurched: the rebirth of "apostolic congregations" across the American mission field* (Nashville, Tennessee: Abingdon Press, 1996), 144.

clergy, can no longer evangelize their communities, and many churches cannot even retain most of their own young people."[9] In spite of these changes, the very foundation of Christian religion will remain. The foundation of Christian religion is faith in the crucified and risen Jesus.

> Christianity cannot ignore its past. It is a historical religion and its originating experience was expressed through interplay of near Eastern cultures in the first century AD. Since then, that experience has received successive cultural expressions in diverse historic cultures. It would therefore be unthinkable that Christian evangelization should not entail the transmission of certain cultural elements from one culture to another, and vice versa.[10]

Christian faith is not based on cultural events nor on cultural influences, but on the life, death, and resurrection of Jesus Christ and his teachings.

2.2 Culture and Religion

Religion and culture are closely connected in human history and civilization. Culture is an integral part of religion, and cultural rituals and cultural practices are the mundane language people use to understand and express their religion. According to Paul Tillich, "Religion as ultimate concern is the meaning-giving substance of culture, and culture is the totality of forms in which the basic concern of religion expressed itself."[11] All religion is connected to its culture. Christianity and its culture are also very closely connected.

> For some Christians and parts of the Christian community Jesus Christ is a great teacher and lawgiver who in what he said of God and the moral law so persuades the mind and will that there is henceforth no escape from him.

---

[9] *Ibid.*, 12.
[10] Shorter, *Toward a Theology of Inculturation*, 57.
[11] Tillich, *Theology of Culture*, 2.

> Christianity is for them a new law and a new religion proclaimed by Jesus.[12]

For some people, Christianity is a new community. But for others, it is a new law and a new religion proclaimed by Jesus.

> For still others Christianity is primarily neither new teaching nor new life but a new community, the Holy Catholic Church; hence the work of Christ which occupies the center of their attention is his founding of this new society which mediates his grace through word and sacrament.[13]

Religion is the search for God. Religious experience is not only the experience of need and desire. It is also the experience of satisfaction. "The search for God tends to produce rapid results; and one could quote innumerable testimonies of converts speaking of the fullness of life into which they have entered."[14] Culture and religion are closely connected, but human relationships vary according to time, region, and people's life style. Often culture is more important to people's life than religion. Culture is all about our past experience in life. Religion is often tied to our future experience in life. Religious patterns and rituals are often influenced by customs, manners, and social behavior of the people. "The symbols of a cultural system are the products of society. They are the components of the mental patterns and pictures through which a society understands and orients itself to life in the world."[15] Our culture influences faith and religion. Culture is an important basic element in our faith beliefs and religion.

Culture changes religion and religious beliefs often reform religion. "If religion is a fundamental mode of cultural behavior, it must be part of the interpretation of life that a culture offers

---

[12] Niebuhr, *Christ and Culture*, 12.
[13] *Ibid.*, 12.
[14] Joly, *What is Faith*, 57.
[15] Shorter, *Toward a Theology of Inculturation*, 35.

its adepts. It must operate in and through a culture. In other words, the beliefs and practices of religion must themselves form a cultural system."[16] The great Protestant Reformation was the result of cultural changes. "When (and assuming) Martin Luther tacked his theses to the door of the church at Wittenberg Castle, he was responding to ecclesial pressures that had been building around his natal form of Christianity and culture for over a century."[17] Culture influences religion and often controls religious faith. Religion operates in and through a culture. The beliefs and practices of religion must themselves form a cultural system. "A cultural system is therefore a configuration of symbols that acts as a bridge between ideas and behavior. Religion itself is such a cultural system."[18] Culture and religion are very closely connected, and culture has a very important role to play in every religion.

In the Christian religion, Jesus Christ is the central affirmation. A Christian is ordinarily defined as "one who believes in Jesus Christ," or "a follower of Jesus Christ."[19] People's customs, ways of living, and manners play an important part in worship and religious beliefs. Every religious ritual is also culturally formed. In this regard, every religion in a particular culture has its own customs and values. In many cultures, religion and culture are so intertwined that the cultural priorities and realities are also religious priorities and realities. In every religious community culture has an important role. Many voices have also raised opinions about the relationship between culture and Christianity or Christianity and culture. Christianity is not only a religion. It is the life of a Christian community. Today more than ever church and culture are

---

[16] *Ibid.*, 40.
[17] Tickle, *The Great Emergence*, 43.
[18] Shorter, *Toward a Theology of Inculturation*, 40.
[19] Niebuhr, *Christ and Culture*, 11.

inseparable in a faith community, and culture is an important part of the church. The Christian church is a worshiping community of the followers of Christ. Faith in Jesus Christ and His teachings are connected to Christian fellowship. But beyond faith, fellowship is also an important part of a religious community life. Culture plays an important role in Christian religion.

Culture plays an important part in every faith community. In Islam, Allah is the center of attention. Prophet Muhammad is not God but is only the messenger of God. Muhammad is the voice of Allah. Islam has a very rich tradition and plays a major role in many cultures. Over the years the Muslim community has contributed many valuable lessons to the world. For Muslims worldwide, their lifestyle, customs, and manners play an important role in their religious belief.

> As Scholars representing a variety of disciplines continue to explore these theories, some American Muslims see in them proof that Islam played a role in the early history of this country. The possibility of such connections with Spanish cultures is particularly appealing to those U.S. Hispanics who are attracted by Islamic teachings.[20]

Over the years, Islam has also played a major role in world history. The impact of Muslims in North America paved the way for the ideological formation of Islam. "Muslim intellectuals and leaders who have become a significant part of the American academic scene have been able to provide an interpretation of Islam relevant to life in the United States as well as to the modern world."[21]

---

[20] Jane I. Smith, *Islam in America* (New York: Columbia University Press, 1999), 51.
[21] Yvonne Yazbeck Haddad, ed., *The Muslims of America* (New York: Oxford University Press, 1991), 4.

2.3 Culture and Christ

In Greek, the word for church, *ekklesia*, means an assembly of people. Culture is often defined as human efforts and experience. "Jesus gave the culture of his days the shock of divine otherness and of eschatological newness. This is why he died, but his resurrection means, for those who follow him, the ever renewed thrust toward others and toward the Other One."[22] In order to understand the gospel, we must understand the message in its cultural background. "For the Jesus Christ of the New Testament is in our actual history, in history as we remember and live it, as it shapes our present faith and action. And this Jesus Christ is a definite person, one and the same whether he appears as man of flesh and blood or as risen Lord."[23] But due to cultural changes we are no longer able to conduct our lives like the people in the first century. Culture provides the information that we base our lives upon. Human beings are culture forming animals and are totally dependent upon their success. Our solutions and decisions are related to our own faith and our religious understandings and beliefs.

> In the case of Jesus, we find a tension or bipolarity between his prophetic stance and his cultural conformity. He is a Jew, a full member of the people of Israel, but he stands often on the fringe of Israelite mainstreams. He is Galilean rather than Judean, a villager rather than a member of the elite of the religious (Jerusalem), administrative (Sepphoris), or economic (Tiberias, Tarichaea) urban centers, an artisan farmer rather than a priest, a scribe, or a political leader. In this sense, he is a "marginal Jew," who stood outside the pale of well-established interpretations of Judaism.[24]

H. Richard Niebuhr, one of the leading theologians of the twentieth century, describes in his book, *Christ and Culture*, five

---

[22] Legrand, *The Bible on Culture*, 174.
[23] Niebuhr, *Christ and Culture*, 13.
[24] Legrand, *The Bible on Culture*, 111.

different ways in which Christ is found to be in relationship with culture. He identifies culture as a social, human achievement that supports values good for human beings. His book begins with describing the enduring problem, which for him is the relationship between Christianity and culture. "When Christianity deals with the question of reason and revelation, what is ultimately in question is the relation of the revelation in Christ to the reason which prevails in culture."[25] Niebuhr's typology is that Christ and culture are competing powers. He presents five different typologies to resolve the problem of competition between Christ and culture.

Niebuhr's first category is "Christ against Culture." This was the general attitude of the early Christian churches. They lived a life away from the world. Even today, this attitude is prevalent within the Charismatic Movement. The movement often ignores the fact that God is present in the world, and God can be experienced in the world. "Christ against Culture" acknowledges the most severe model of thought that denies any relationship between the Trinity and the world. "A proper Trinitarian understanding will keep these various dimensions of Divine concern in constant balance; the Father and the Sprit, each in some sense on the side of culture, must not be forgotten in unique concentration upon the (anti-cultural) demands of the Son."[26]

Niebuhr's second type is "Christ of Culture." This category has led to the accommodation of Christ to culture. Jesus Christ as the Messiah, not only for the early Christians, but also for the people of all generations, strengthens this argument. This attitude has produced a "Culture-Protestantism," which has

---

[25] Niebuhr, *Christ and Culture*, 11.
[26] Glen H. Stassen, D.M. Yeager, and John Howard Yoder, *Authentic Transformation* (Nashville: Abingdon Press, 1996), 35.

been characterized by a desire to bring Christ and culture together. This type was represented in the Hellenistic world by the Christian Gnostics. This type also faced strong criticism from pagan writers as well as from the orthodox. Marxists also dislike Christian socialism as much as the **Orthodox** and the Lutherans. "If as Niebuhr indicates at one point, 'culture' is what the New Testament refers to as 'the world,' then it becomes obvious that one of the 'types' of answer to the question we are studying will be to expect a clear and abiding conflict between Christ and culture."[27]

His third typology has set "Christ above Culture." The teaching of Christ to sell everything for His sake, to turn the other cheek to the violent, to humble ourselves and become the servants of all, to abandon family and not to worry about tomorrow, all strengthen this position. These arguments are also not without critique. There are many statements in the gospel arguing for the position of Christ and culture. "Do not think that I have come to abolish the law or the prophets; I have come not to abolish but to fulfill" (Matthew 5:17, NRSV). Critics also argue that Jesus is the son of God who created the heaven and the earth.

Niebuhr's fourth typology, "Christ and Culture in Paradox," presents a prohibition for relationship that is based on the categorical differences between Jesus and humanity. This type represents the loyalties of human beings to God and nature. Loyalty to nature also involves sin against God. According to this type, there is no escape from sin, and a person must live not by his righteousness but by the continual forgiveness of God. "The question about Christ and culture in this situation is not one which man puts to himself, but one that God asks him; it is not a question about Christians and

---

[27] *Ibid.*, 34.

pagans, but a question about God and man."[28] This seems to be the most realistic of the several attitudes necessary for Christian life. "Grace is in God, and sin is in man. The grace of God is not a substance, a manalike power, which is mediated to men through human acts. Grace is always in God's action; it is God's attribute."[29] This view is represented by Paul, Marcion, Luther, and others.

> The obvious shortcoming of this approach, according to Niebuhr, is that the lack of any constitutive link between Law and Grace, since they do not operate on the same level, means that there can be no clear way of guiding the Christian's discriminating choices about action on the level of culture.[30]

Niebuhr's fifth category, "Christ the Transformer of Society," is one of power, for here he emphasized Jesus' participation in the renewal of creation. This view extends redemption, not only to individuals, but also to the human culture. The nature of humanity is corrupted, but it is not inherently bad. Corruption can be purified and culture can be converted. "The kingdom of God is transformed culture, because it is first of all the conversion of the human spirit from faithlessness and self service to the knowledge and service of God."[31] As Christ the transformer of cultures, He firmly establishes the participation of the Word, the Son of God, in the ongoing creative act of God. In the other categories Christ is either separate from, or identified with the prevailing culture. "This double affirmation of nature and of history, which we may note is cognate to the earlier discussion of the work of the Father and of the Holy Spirit, explains the claim that the 'transformationist' position is more complete and balanced than any of the others."[32]

---

[28] Niebuhr, *Christ and Culture*, 150.
[29] *Ibid..* 151.
[30] Stassen, *Authentic Transformation*, 39.
[31] Niebuhr, *Christ and Culture*, 228.
[32] Stassen, *Authentic Transformation*, 40.

Niebuhr's five typologies are helpful in understanding the relationship between Christ and culture but have limitations. Critique against culture fails to understand human sinfulness in the heart, rather than in the culture. There are many statements in the Gospels arguing for the position of Christ and culture. Critiques of "Christ above Culture" have called for Niebuhr to give attention to concrete criteria and cases. Niebuhr's type of "Christ and Culture in Paradox" represents the loyalties of human beings to God and nature. Protestants who argue for law and grace represent this position. In this view, whatever work human beings are engaged in this temporal world, they are still filled with sin, and grace is the gift of God. In order to understand the gospel, we must understand the cultural background of Jesus Christ. Culture is the pattern of behavior and a simple system that can be visible in our life. Culture provides the information upon which we base our lives. "Hence belief in Jesus Christ by men in their various cultures always means belief in God. No one can know the Son without acknowledging the Father."[33] Niebuhr, in conclusion, is saying that throughout Christian history the Christian community has employed a diversity of responses to the competing powers of Christ and culture. Culture is part of Jesus' ministry and the Church cannot be separated from society. Christ is seen as opposed to the customs of the dominant society, but Jesus often appears as part of the society and culture. Niebuhr's preference is for *Christ the Transformer of Culture* position as the most realistic position that a Christian can take.

> In our time answers of this kind are given by Christians who note the close relation between Christianity and Western civilization, between Jesus' teachings or the teachings about him and democratic institutions; yet there are occasional interpretations that emphasize the agreement

---

[33] Niebuhr, *Christ and Culture*, 27-28.

between Christ and Eastern culture as well as some that tend to identify him with the spirit of Marxian society.[34]

Jesus' humanity was a product of the culture, but he ignored everything concerned with material civilization. Jesus' humanity was Jewish, but he confronted Jewish culture. "Jesus Christ and God the Father, the gospel, the church, and eternal life may find places in the cultural complex, but only as elements in the great pluralism."[35]

Christianity is a religion of followers of Christ. Niebuhr sums it up very well:

> A Christian is ordinarily defined as 'one who believes in Jesus Christ' or as 'a follower of Jesus Christ'. He might more adequately be described as one who counts himself as belonging to that community of men for whom Jesus Christ—his life, words, deeds, and destiny—is of supreme importance as the key to the understanding of themselves and their world, the main source of the knowledge of God and man, good and evil, the constant companion of the conscience, and the expected deliverer from evil.[36]

Jesus' message made great changes in the lives of the people.

Christ and culture have many different approaches and interpretations, but one thing is sure, that culture is an integral part of every worshiping community. Christian practices and faith are very much influenced by the culture in which the church is situated. As social beings we are all attached to society and culture. "The culture in which any of us are raised seems 'natural' to us, so we would naturally extend 'our kind' of Christianity everywhere unless we know how important it is to adapt to other cultures."[37] In many respects, it is not faith that determines our affiliation to the church, but our culture.

---

[34] *Ibid.*, 41.
[35] Niebuhr, *Christ and Culture*, 38.
[36] *Ibid.*, 11.
[37] Hunter, *Church for the Unchurched*, 61.

Culture

The church is the Community of the new being. Again and again, people say, "I do not like organized religion." The church is not organized religion. It is not hierarchical authority. It is not a social organization. It is all of this, of course, but it is primarily a group of people who express a new reality by which they have been grasped.[38]

2.4 Culture and Bible

The Bible is a product of culture. The Bible presents the culture of a community that lived centuries ago. It reveals the culture of a community over many years. "Further, one can view the Bible as a producer of culture as well as a product of it. The New Testament itself is already a product of the cultural development in Israel over fifteen hundred years of history."[39] It also produces the culture of a community over many years. "The Jewish and Christian Scriptures went on to have a powerful influence on the developing cultures of Europe and the Mediterranean rim. In the nineteenth and twentieth centuries, missionary movements touched cultures beyond this geographic region in a dramatic way."[40]

One of the most inspiring aspects of the Bible as a religious book is its feeling of freshness to everyday readers. Throughout the centuries, biblical teachings have been relevant in every community and culture. One of the main reasons for this is many of the biblical laws and teachings resonate in human history and civilization. Many biblical laws came from ancient laws and were part of ancient cultures. Biblical teachings and laws are also connected to human history and culture. For example, the Ten Commandments are the basis for Christian principles. The Ten Commandments are also known as the basis of human laws. These laws are revered and observed by

---

[38] Tillich, *Theology of Culture*, 212.
[39] Legrand, *The Bible on Culture*, vii.
[40] *Ibid.*

Christians as their own. They were given to the Israelites through Moses over 3000 years ago on Mount Sinai by Yahweh. Yahweh gave these laws to the Israelites to restore order and stability in a society when it was socially and morally decaying. These laws were given not only to restore religious faith in God but also to establish an orderly life-supporting society. They continue to be the basis of social and ethical order in the society. The ethical principles of the Ten Commandments can be traced back to the life of the Israelite patriarchs. "The Lord said to Moses, 'Cut two tablets of stone like the former ones, and I will write on the tablets the words that were on the former tablets, which you broke'" (Ex.34:1). "The ten commandments are more than archaic demands, underneath are principles of love, honor, justice and respect. The principles are given in the context of covenant and are bound to the passion for liberation found in the Exodus narrative."[41]

Now there is clear evidence to suggest that these commandments have some connection to the ancient laws of the society. The basic characteristic of the Ten Commandments is that they are prohibitions by themselves without any explanations. This has led some to believe that the Ten Commandments may have some connection between ancient religious laws or accepted civil laws of the ancient society. The Sumerians, the Babylonians, the Assyrians, and other people of Mesopotamia from ancient times influenced nearly every legal system of the world. "The resemblance between the Ten Commandments and, for example, the Code of Hammurabi is so high, both formally and with regard to content that I find it inappropriate to speak of the Decalogue as a law code."[42]

---

[41] Ronald E. Vallet, *The Steward Living in Covenant* (Grand Rapids, Michigan: William B. Eerdmans Publishing Company, 2001), 229.
[42] Walter Harrelson, *The Ten Commandments and Human Rights* (Philadelphia: Fortress Press, 1980), 22.

Nothing definite can be said regarding the Ten Commandments except to suggest that these commandments have many similarities to civil laws.

The Sinai covenant relationship of the Ten Commandments resembles many ancient religious rules and moral codes. Stipulations of obligations in the Hittite suzerainty-vassal treaties are very similar to the Ten Commandments. "The form of the Sinai covenant as it appears in the Deuteronomic story resembles Hittite suzerainty-vassal treaties of the fourteenth and thirteenth centuries B.C.E and Assyrian treaties of the seventh and sixth centuries BCE."[43] Similar moral codes and covenant treaties can be traced to many religions of ancient times. The Exodus details of the Ten Commandments may be the first known set of rules and regulations in the history of Israel. But the Ten Commandments are not by any means the oldest known covenant stories in history. "If Moses is to be credited with a component of the Ten Commandments, he may be identified with the first and second commandments. He is certainly responsible for the exclusivistic Yahwism that generated them, whether or not the actual wording can be attributed to him."[44] The most important difference between the Commandment Laws and the laws which existed in the ancient period is the ancient laws are mere conditional ordinances, but the commandments are unconditional laws. "The covenant code is an application of the fundamental principles of the Ten Commandments to specific matters of daily conduct."[45]

---

[43] Henry Jackson Flanders, Robert Wilson Crapps, and David Anthony Smith, *People of the Covenant* (New York: Oxford University Press, Inc., 1996), 198. (This year is listed differently from the bibliography. My quote is from 1996 version. OK)
[44] Dale Patrick, *Old Testament Law* (Louisville, Kentucky: John Knox Press, 1985), 40.
[45] Flanders, *People of the Covenant*, 203.

The Ten Commandments are regarded as the basis of morality in the civilized world. Many aspects of the laws of the Ten Commandments are still suitable for modern society. Undoubtedly, ancient religious laws are the foundation and basis of the moral values of modern society. But in recent years many of these laws have come under heavy attack by those who say that these laws have no place in contemporary society. Their validity is in question in the modern world after many years of experience and acceptance. It is doubtful whether human history has witnessed such rapid changes in society as the twentieth century. During the past century, people's lives and cultures have changed so much and so rapidly. Many aspects of the Ten Commandment laws are no longer applicable to the people's relationship to God and neighbors. For example, the fourth commandment is regarding the Sabbath day to remember God's creative action in our life. **"Observe the Sabbath day and keep it holy, as the Lord your God commanded you." (Deut. 5:12, NRSV) The seventh day is marked as Sabbath day holy time for God as well as resting time for the human body.** "But the seventh day is a sabbath to the Lord your God; you shall not do any work—you, or your son or your daughter, or your male or female slave, or your ox or your donkey, or any of your livestock, or the resident alien in your towns, so that your male and female slave may rest as well as you" (Deut. 5:14-26, NRSV). Some people's lives have changed so much in the modern world that it is impossible to keep the Sabbath day as a resting day. Most people's lifestyle has also changed; they no longer have an ox or a donkey or any other livestock in their possession. Keeping male or female slaves is no more a civilized or legal option. But the basic principle of the law will remain intact as long as human beings exist.

The Ten Commandments and similar types of law are essential for the existence of a civilized world. The Bible stands very much for basic human rights, and the Ten Commandment

Culture 31

laws play a major role in keeping human rights and dignity. In that regard, the commandment laws are part of every culture and every civilization. Religion and religious beliefs are part of every culture and society. Indeed, religious laws and culture are closely related. Neither can exist without being separated from the other. The Bible will always be relevant to human needs. Laws similar to the Ten Commandments originated in culture and became part of the Bible. Every culture needs religion and all religions are an essential part of every culture.

Biblical culture has greatly influenced biblical teachings. Slavery was part of the culture of the biblical period. Culture changed during the centuries, and for the modern world slavery is one of the shameful acts of any society. "Because the business of one person's owning another person is neither morally defensible nor economically sensible in an industrialized society, we got over this major blow to sola scriptura."[46] Women's role in society, their freedom, and divorce were controversial issues of biblical teaching. But for the modern world these are important justice issues for Christians to tackle. When the stories of abuse and horror come out from families, society comes out strongly supporting divorce. Religion and culture are closely connected and often cultural beliefs have merged with religious beliefs. The Bible is part of this classic matrix.

2.5 Culture and Society

Throughout the centuries, culture and society have been closely connected. Religion and culture were always influenced by society and the social behavior of people. Family system in the Eastern culture has been in existence for over two thousand years. It is mainly rooted in the patriarchal system of society. Social norms in the Western culture are not always the same

---

[46] Tickle, *The Great Emergence*, 99.

as in the Eastern culture. Often social norms are religious and cultural norms. For example, open friendship between same sexes in eastern countries is not automatically considered a homosexual relation: "It is not unusual to see two men in close embrace or two women with arms around each other in public places. (In fact, it is often more difficult for a heterosexual couple to publicly express their affection for each other!)."[47] On the other hand, in India and the East, in general, friendship between unmarried couples of the opposite sex is not accepted either socially or legally. Embracing in public between opposite sexes and other acts or expressions of love in public are not socially accepted and have legal implications in the Eastern culture. Dating and other western forms of marriage arrangements are still not a part of accepted practices in the Eastern culture. Arranged marriages and the seclusion of opposite sexes and other social practices in society are still considered common in Eastern cultures. In India, marriage is a relationship between two families, rather than two individuals. In the marriage relationship, most often, family will have the final word. Society also plays an important role in the marriage relationship.

Women were considered an object of sexuality. "Purda"[48] and other practices of hiding women from the public are still strict customs of Islamic culture. Many of these traditions originated in culture in order to protect women in the society. Now they are part and parcel of the religious community. Christian communities in the eastern countries are also indebted to many of these cultural practices. In Indian Christian

---

[47] Aruna Gnanadason, "The Struggle to be Human: A Reflection on Homosexuality in India". *Other Voices, Other Worlds.* ed. Terry Brown, (New York: Church Publishing Incorporated, 2006), 79.

[48] Purda is a system of keeping women out of the sight of men other than their immediate family members, commonly practiced in Islamic countries where women cover their entire body before going out in public.

Culture 33

communities, wine, beer, and other alcoholic drinks are considered to be sin. Living together before marriage is not an accepted practice or an option in Indian culture. It is also illegal under the Indian legal system to have a relationship between unmarried couples. In this context, it is an important issue for the church to have a contextual theology for people of different cultures.

God did not make man and woman at the same time in the story of the Garden of Eden. In some places, the Bible gives a superior status to men over women. In the Creation story in Genesis 2, God made woman as a helper to man: "It is not good that the man should be alone; I will make him a helper as his partner" (Gen. 2:18, NRSV). Some may argue a superior status of men over women: "Although we may argue with some success that the Garden of Eden does not really make woman subject to man, it is impossible to argue that St. Paul does not operate from that principle."[49] Undoubtedly, there was a clear distinction between men and women in biblical culture. It is often not the ability but the traditions and customs that played a part in the role of women in the New Testament. Women had an important role in the early churches. They financially aided Jesus and the disciples. They celebrated the Lord's Supper in remembrance of how Jesus had delivered them from sin. They expressed their hope for the day when the Christ will come again.

Women in the New Testament were responsible and efficient in managing their homes even though much of the writing suggests that they were under the supervision and guidance of their husbands. In many places in the Bible, we see images of women running their households while their husbands saw to civic affairs outside the home.

---

[49] Tickle, *The Great Emergence*, 99.

> In the text Socrates, in conversation with Xenophon, sees the husband and wife acting as partners (koinonoi) in the household. Property comes in largely through the husband's activity and is dispensed through the wife's activity, so that she contributes an equally important (antirropon) service toward its success. [50]

House church was the center of prayer and evangelization. Women played a leading role in the house church. Women were committed and faithful. Women were also leading contributors to the early church. Priscilla, Aquila contributed not only their houses, but also their entire assets for the service of the gospel. Women were also good at visiting the sick and the imprisoned, the kinds of activity we expect of Christians: "I was sick and you took care of me, I was in prison and you visited me" (Matthew 25:36, NRSV).). There are plenty of examples of houses led by women in the New Testament: "As soon as he realized this, he went to the house of Mary, the mother of John whose other name was Mark, where many had gathered and were praying" (Acts 12:12, NRSV).). "Neither was man created for the sake of woman, but woman for the sake of man. For this reason a woman ought to have a symbol of authority on her head" (1 Cor. 11:9, 10, NRSV).). Women were not equal partners in the New Testament society. Throughout the Bible we see discriminating phrases used against women. "The character of the culture makes it unlikely that all such religious instruction took place in mixed groups."[51]

The **recognition** given to women for their contribution is not noteworthy. Male dominated biblical society purposefully ignored the importance of women in the formation of the early church. Their culture informed their thinking. Many important

---

[50] Carolyn Osiek, Margaret Y. Macdonald with Janet H. Tulloch, *A Woman's Place: House Churches in Earliest Christianity* (Minneapolis: Fortress Press, 2006), 146.

[51] Carolyn Osiek, *A Woman's Place*, 13.

gospel stories written by women are not part of the Bible, not because they lack importance, but because of women's status in the New Testament culture. The New Testament code of conduct often conveys to modern readers a rather passive submission of wife to husband. It was not because of a biblical attitude, but because of the society and culture of the time. In the ancient patriarchal culture the status of women was inferior to men.

Until the twentieth century, even mainline Protestant denominations did not widely accept women for ordination. "Although a few Protestant groups ordained women in the nineteenth century, it is not until the mid-1950s to 1970s that most major American protestant denominations ordained women."[52] Some would argue that when American women were allowed ordination in Protestant churches, it was not because of biblical teaching, but due to the pressure of society and culture.[53] It was not a religious solution, but it was welcoming news for many communities. Not only are women called to the priesthood today, they are also elevated to the episcopacy.

The role of women in different cultures is also very different even within this century.

> Some would claim that in traditional Mediterranean cultures the only real honor for a woman is that of her family and its dominant males, while for her there is only appropriate sensitivity to shame, expressed in shyness and sexual exclusivity. For others, women bear the responsibility for guarding not only family but national honor, and the honor of women is that of the family.[54]

---

[52] Rosemary Ruether, *Sexism and God-Talk* (Boston: Beacon Press Books, 1993), 199.
[53] Tickle, *The Great Emergence*, 99-101.
[54] Carolyn Osiek, *A Woman's Place*, 7.

Even today in many parts of the world women are regarded as second class citizens. There is a clear distinction between female and male roles in the society. In many cultures women are considered to be inferior to men. In many religions women are not treated equally in all matters. The veiling of women is still a custom in Islamic countries. "The task for us is to find those forms which will express our human identity in ways which are culturally appropriate."[55] In other dominant religions in India, especially Hinduism, women are still forbidden from the role of priesthood. The Catholic Church still does not allow women's ordination. It is certainly not because of their lack of ability, leadership, or faith, but only because of their gender. In Indian culture women have different roles. In home and society they are considered second to men, but in political leadership they enjoy important positions. Over the centuries, many courageous women have played leading roles in Indian history. Rani of Jhansi, Indira Gandhi, and Sonia Gandhi are a few who can never be forgotten. On the other hand, women are still playing a second class role in the Indian family and religious society. Women's ordination in India is still very rare and not widely accepted even in the Church of South India. **It is mainly due to the women's place in Indian culture and culture.** Hindu joint family system, culture, and tradition have an important role for women in the family and religious circle.

If women could play a leading role in the early church and contribute significantly to the growth of Christianity, they should also now assume leadership roles in the church and enter into priesthood. If women can be good doctors and manage households, they can undoubtedly also manage church administration and worship services. Cultures have had a

---

[55] Sr. Vandana, "Water – God's Extravaganza: John 2.1-11"*Voices From the Margin: Interpreting the Bible in the Third World*, ed. R.S. Sugirtharajah, (Maryknoll, New York: Orbis Books, 1995), 195.

Culture 37

profound impact on the role women play in the church, and while the Bible clearly shows a distinction between male and female, this fact is due to the culture of the time. **Women's role in the Jewish law and custom were very limited. But Jesus questioned many of the Jewish laws and the practices.** "Do not think that I have come to abolish the law or the prophets; I have come not to abolish but to fulfill." (Mathew 5:17, NRSV) **Jesus treated women as equal to men. Women played an import role in Jesus ministry. Many of His close advisors were women. "The twelve were with him, as well as some women who had been cured of evil spirits and infirmities: Mary, called Magdalene, from whom seven demons had gone out and Joanna, the wife of Herod's steward Chuza, and Susanna, and many others, who provided for them out of their resources." (Luke 8:1-3, NRSV) He also appeared first to women after His resurrection.** The role of women in society and in religious life is part of culture. God created women with many advantages over men. Child birth is one of the most important abilities God has given only to women.

Human sexuality is another major issue in the Western world that is at odds with the Eastern culture and values. There is ample evidence in the Old Testament to show that the origin of the issue is as old as human history. The two Creation accounts in the book of Genesis, "So God created humankind in his image, in the image of God he created them; male and female he created them" (Gen. 1:26-27); and "Therefore a man leaves his father and his mother and clings to his wife, and they become one flesh" (Gen. 2:24), are fundamental to the discussion about homosexuality in the church. In India, due to social shame people are afraid to come out of their closet: "But then, in the Indian context, there is a large percentage of adults who would engage in both heterosexual and homosexual relationships. Unwritten family codes force most to hide their homosexual identity or express it only surreptitiously."⁵⁶ Human sexuality is one of the major issues facing the Christian community in the Western world today. While sexual orientation is now a polarizing issue in the West, it is still not an issue in India, either in the society or in religious circles, because of the traditional social and religious practices in the Eastern world. In Western society and culture, homosexuality is not only a sexual issue but an economic one. Living together has a bearing on social and economic affairs in the West, but in some Eastern cultures, particularly in India, homosexuality is not an issue because the existence and rights of homosexuals as human beings are ignored. Homosexual behavior is not accepted in many religions. In India homosexuality is a punishable offense. "India is one of the few countries that keep this archaic law on sodomy in its law book."⁵⁷ One reason is because India has a large Muslim population. In Muslim religion and culture homosexual behavior is unacceptable. "Although many countries have abandoned the death penalty, homosexual behavior remains illegal in most Islamic societies and in most multi-faith regions with large population of Muslims."⁵⁸

In recent years, homosexuality has become a part of the social culture in the Western world. In the Anglican Communion, it has been a major preoccupation in recent years. Anglican churches in North America embraced and accepted the practice of homosexuality and consecrated an openly homosexual bishop; but their counterparts in the worldwide communion cannot tolerate such practice. The gay and lesbian issue is rocking the Episcopal wing of the Anglican Church in North America. The Episcopal churches in many parts of North

---

⁵⁶ Gnanadason, *The Struggle to Be Human*, 79.
⁵⁷ *Ibid.*, 85.
⁵⁸ *Ibid.*, 116.

Culture 39

America have begun to break away from their denomination in North America and started to join the worldwide Anglican Communion, which is opposed to homosexual practices: "Of all the fights, the gay one must be-has to be-the bitterest, because once it is lost, there are no more fights to be had. It is finished."[59] Homosexuality is already part of the culture. It is a fight to continue in the religious community.

While debate over the issues surrounding homosexuality will not go away in the West, homosexuality is still against the law in many parts of the Eastern world. One of the reasons for the formation and existence of the Church of South India and Marthoma Church, a partner church of the Episcopal Church in North America, is not due to theological reasons, but because of socio-cultural issues.

2.6 Culture and Mission

One of the goals of the Christian church is mission. "Go therefore and make disciples of all nations, baptizing them in the name of the Father and of the Son and of the Holy Spirit, and teaching them to obey everything that I have commanded you" (Matthew 28:19-20). There are two important elements in mission, the message and the messenger, and its understanding in the socio-cultural context. "The essential thing in mission education is the creation of a Christian atmosphere in its institutions."[60] The message of Christian mission is the same everywhere, yesterday, today, and tomorrow, but the messenger must adapt and be different according to cultural relativity.

> In our mission, we are not called to surrender or compromise this way in which Christians perceive reality.

---

[59] Tickle, *The Great Emergence*, 101.
[60] V.S. Azariah, *Christ in Indian Villages* (London: SCM Press, 1930), 113.

> Indeed, Christ commissions us to communicate our most central truth claims to people who do not yet wear New Testament lenses, knowing that Christian conversion involves (in part) the putting on of those lenses and the transformation of one's worldview. The truth is not negotiable.[61]

God created this world in many different shapes and forms. In this world there are many cultures originating from the geography of the area and variety of people's lifestyles, but Christ's presence is in all parts of the world. Christ is present in all global cultures and civilizations.

Culture had an important role in the mission work of the early churches. Christian mission in this world is to translate Christ in the form of people's understanding. "Human beings are deeply tied to culture and cannot be evangelized unless they are addressed in terms of their culture. The Gospel itself cannot be known except through the medium of culture."[62] The role of the church as a mission church will not be a success without a proper understanding of the people it serves. Jesus Christ must be transmitted and translated to the world according to people's own culture and civilization. The Christian message to suffering people must be communicated, not from the palace, but from within the society where suffering is present. Christian mission must learn from the life and work of Jesus Christ. The Messiah was not born in a place of luxury. Jesus Christ was not born in a palace but in a stable. Although it was the people's expectation that the Messiah would be born in a palace, He identified with the poor and the suffering. In order for the missional message to be understood it must be immersed in the people's culture. Christian mission must identify with the culture, identify with the people, and know

---

[61] Hunter, *Church for the Unchurched*, 64-65.
[62] Shorter, *Toward a Theology of Inculturation*, 27.

Culture

their sufferings and joys. Christ must be the center of Christian mission all over the world. Western missionaries often find resistance from eastern countries, not because of their religion, but because of their culture. In order for a foreign religion to survive in any country it is very important that it adopt and adapt to the local culture and social values.

Missionaries must understand the culture and values of the mission field where they are working.

> But the outer forms through which the Truth is communicated are negotiable, and that is the second major insight that should guide our way. To reach an undisciplined population, the forms of outreach, ministry, and worship must be indigenous to their culture, because each people's culture is the natural medium of God's revelation to them.[63]

One of the main techniques of a successful mission is adapting to one's environment and culture. The same can be seen in the example, teaching, and ministry of Saint Paul. Adaptation became more effective when the gospel was preached in a different culture and environment. Missionaries must be willing to listen and learn from people of other faith traditions and cultures in order for their mission work to be successful. "Christian evangelization is an invitation to the people of the culture to respond in freedom at the deepest level of religious meaning."[64]

Many missionaries failed in their mission work in India because they failed to realize the value of the culture in their mission work. During the seventeenth century, Christian missionaries in India were confronted by the rigid Hindu caste system. Robert de Nobili, a missionary to India in 1620, understood clearly and practiced the principles of adaptation. His mission in India was a success because his mission was

---

[63] Hunter, *Church for the Unchurched*, 65.
[64] Shorter, *Toward a Theology of Inculturation*, 55.

one of adaptation, adaptation of Indian culture and social values. His mission was focused among the high class Hindu society, so he adopted a lifestyle of high class Hindus. He learned their language, Tamil, in order to communicate with them. He assumed the customs and lifestyle of the native Indian people in order to work among them. He lived in huts and implemented local rites and ceremonies for the ceremonies of the church. He built an Indian style church. He adopted the food, clothing, and daily routine of the Brahmin *sanyasis* in order to earn their respect for his mission. **Nobili's adaptation did not stop with food and clothing; he even tried to look like a local Brahmin by fixing his hair (*kudumbi*), wearing Brahminical thread and wearing only sandals. Brahmins are high class Hindus and they inherit the birth right to be Hindu priests. Fixing hair in a special way keeping few long ones, wearing a thread across the body and wearing only sandals are some of the well known practices of Brahmins identifying them self from others. He also carried a water jug with him like a high caste Brahmin.** Mostly he remained in solitude and in yogic posture like them. He claimed to be one among them, and his status as one among them gave him enormous entry and privilege all over India. He understood completely the value of culture and civilization. He changed the names of saints and worship places to sound like Hindu temples. His effort was to adapt Christianity to the local Indians. His idea was good, but he often went too far to gain acceptance. He was a man who understood completely the value of culture in mission. "The word of God as it is uttered to men comes in human words; and human words are cultural things, along with the concepts with which they are associated."[65]

Robert de Nobili's mission work was a success in India in many respects because he knew well the critical value of culture

---

[65] Niebuhr, *Christ and Culture*, 104.

in the mission field. **"Nobili's great work was his opening the door for the Gospel. The baptisms he gave may not be thousands, but the method he followed brought thousands."**[66] He was a model representative for missionary work in a different cultural environment. But his lifestyle was controversial in many circles. He supported the caste system and caste marks and adopted the high caste Brahmin customs of sandal paste, *kudumbi*, frequent baths, **Brahminical** thread, etc. He also did not discourage local customs and discrimination because his main aim was to convert local people to Christianity. While he adopted the high caste customs to get respect among the society, he worked among the low caste during the night and converted many to Christianity.[67] His aim was to convert local people to Christianity, but in order to get the support of the powerful high class community he pretended to be one among them. He worked among the low caste during night cover because of the reality of untouchable practices among the castes.

Like in other Eastern societies, Indian culture and religion are so intertwined that cultural realities also become religious realities. Many of the social problems in India can be traced to religious causes. Christian mission in India must be the culture of the Dalit, and the poor in India. **In the midst of the Dalit and the poor, it is only through the liberation of them that God becomes manifest to them.** The role of Christian mission is important in the struggle to transform the society where the presence of Christ can be grasped and seen. Niebuhr calls it "Christ the Transformer of Culture." Society is not in need of replacement, but of transformation. "The good nature of man has been corrupted and his culture has become perverse in such

---

[66] S. Rajamanickam, "Roberto de Nobili and Adaptation", *Indian Church history Review* 1 (November 1967), 91.
[67] *Ibid.*, 83.

fashion that corrupt nature produces perverse culture and perverse culture corrupts nature."[68] The corrupted nature of the human being makes the transformation of culture impossible for him, but he looks to Christ as the "possibility of the impossible." "For God so loved the world that he gave his only son, so that everyone who believes in him may not perish but may have eternal life" (John 3:16, NRSV).).

Cultural realities are also religious realities in all societies, particularly in all suffering societies. "Of these, life, humanity, reason, society, and culture are not only powers but also values, goods to which we have been attached by a necessary love."[69] The problems of the Dalit community in India are not the individuals, but the society the individuals are a part of. Dalits in India have suffered in the past, and they continue to suffer in the present. This is not because of their sins or the sins of their ancestors.

> God's divinity and his humanity are both characterized by his dalitness. His dalitness is the key to the mystery of his divine human unity. He is one with the broken. He suffers when his people suffer. He weeps when his people weep. He laughs when his people laugh. He dies in his people's death, raised again in his people's resurrection.[70]

The role of Christian mission in such a Dalit context is the role of Christ the Liberator. "And the response to the Gospel cannot be mere passive understanding or acceptance or mystical experience; it means sharing in the love of Christ, and passing on that love to the world, in active, loving service and suffering."[71] When society hears the voice of Christ, and love

---

[68] Niebuhr, *Christ and Culture*, 211.

[69] *Ibid.*, 250.

[70] A.P. Nirmal, *Towards a Christian Dalit Theology in Frontiers in Asian Christian Theology*, ed. R.S.Sugirtharaja (Maryknoll, New York: Orbis Books, 1994), 230.

[71] Robin Boyd, *An Introduction to Indian Christian Theology* (Delhi, India: ISPCK, 1969), 330.

and justice are practiced, then transformation will occur in the community, and Christian mission will be a meaningful one for God's creation. The lack of growth of Christianity in Asia is due to the misdirected focus of mission and not because of the content of the message of Christ.

Christian mission and culture are closely connected, and culture has a major role to play in any mission work. Successful mission work cannot ignore the critical value of culture. Human history has taught us that in order for mission to be effective it cannot ignore the human experience and must work within the culture of a community.

2.7 Culture and Ministry

Our ministry at St. Columba Episcopal Church in Hanover Park, Illinois, is a fine example of culture and its relevance to a worshiping community. I started my ministry at St. Columba as an Anglican minister. At St. Columba's we hoped that Anglican members from all over the world would join us for worship. It is quite logical to think that way because of the particularities of the worship service in the Anglican community worldwide. During the last two years, many worldwide Anglicans came to visit us and worship with us along with our Anglo-American community. But most visitors were not comfortable worshiping with Anglo-Americans even though I was their priest.

Once St. Columba was a prominent church in the Episcopal Diocese of Chicago because of its location and its financial stability, but in recent years membership has declined to a handful. At present, we are struggling financially to make both ends meet. As a church we are serving the local community in many ways, and the community is also very much appreciative of our ministry. Our local community is changing, and people of all nations are members of our community now. My original goal as the priest of St. Columba was to attract membership from the multicultural community of Hanover Park. My goal is to make disciples for Christ from all nations.

St. Columba Episcopal Church is a beautiful Episcopal (Anglican) Church in the western suburb of Chicago. The church sits on four acres of land, surrounded by beautiful trees. The building is small, but very beautiful in appearance, with a traditional Anglican altar and setting. Since it has a high church background, there are many traditional icons and decorations in the sanctuary. Our church can accommodate over one hundred people in the worship hall. It also has a large fellowship hall downstairs along with many separate rooms for Sunday School and other activities. Our worship hall and fellowship hall have separate entrances on the ground floor, so it can be used for different activities simultaneously. The ministry location of our church is well suited for many ministries and has promising potential for expansion and growth. Its setting is also well suited for multicultural ministry because St. Columba is surrounded by many ethnic groups. On weekdays the church is open for many different community activities. During the last two years, the church has gained a new outlook, and our members have gained a new attitude in welcoming others. During **the past one year** of my ministry we have overcome many of our shortcomings and focused on our goal to grow and thrive. The members of our church are predominantly white. In my short period of ministry, I have observed that people have become more cooperative and willing to accept others into their fellowship.

Our original goal was to make a multicultural worshipping community. Our effort was to invite, proclaim, and share Jesus Christ with those who are Hispanic, African, Asian and the other people God loves from multi-national communities. We have opened the church to serve many multicultural ministries. I knew well that culture is an integral part of the church and cultural fellowship has an important role in the church.

Understanding the value of community and culture in the faith community, we became involved in many Hanover Park community activities last year. We participated in the city carnival and parade. As a faith community we are always available for all the emergency needs of the city and the township, such needs as helping flood victims, feeding the hungry, and helping the poor. **Our church is open throughout the week for programs and meetings of groups like the Alcoholics Anonymous, food program at the Hanover Park food pantry, Backpack Buddies for school supplies and Veterans of Foreign Wars and others.** We are also designated as an emergency shelter for crisis programs of the city, township, and the state. As a church we provide food for the homeless, and we support and work at the community homeless shelter. Our church membership may be small, but we are always willing to go and be in the forefront to help others during their crisis.

Last year, as an area priest, I also helped the community in many ways. As an Asian priest, I am active in the Asian American ministry of the Episcopal Church. This year we hosted an Asian clergy family get together at St. Columba. I am also very active in the Ecumenical Council of Kerala Churches in greater Chicago. Last year we celebrated our Silver Jubilee, and they chose me as the co-coordinator for the Jubilee programs. We have worked very closely with the multicultural leadership community. We hope that these wider community activities and programs will give us more visibility in and around the Hanover Park community, which might attract more members of other ethnic groups to our worship and fellowship community.

We have also started community worship services. Once a month we have an Episcopal worship service at a nearby retirement community called Friendship Village.[72] During the last year, seven to twelve Episcopal residents of that community regularly and enthusiastically took part in that service. A few members from our church also attend that service on a regular basis. Frequently, I assist at St. Mark Episcopal Church during their Wednesday services and other special occasions. We are also engaged in many joint activities with the nearby ELCA-Living Christ Lutheran Church. **On August** 10, 2008), we had a successful joint picnic with the Living Christ Lutheran Church. In spite of all our efforts, Sunday attendance of Asians and Hispanics from the surrounding area is still very low. The multicultural ministry we had hoped for did not materialize because Asians and Hispanics preferred their own ethnic community for worship and fellowship. We welcomed many communities to our midst. Many from different cultures showed up for different worship services, but only very few chose St. Columba as their home.

Culture indeed played an important part in worship, and many who came by to visit our church felt that reality among them. As a priest from a different culture and as one among them, I hoped that I would be more acceptable to the multicultural groups of people, but cultural fellowship was an important part for many of them. We have not stopped our efforts, but we know that it will be hard for the first generation of immigrants to mingle with the Anglican community of a different culture. Culture in fellowship is an important part of the church. We made many efforts to invite new ethnic groups into our church fellowship. However, many of the new

---

[72] FriendshipVillage is one of the largest retirement communities near our church.

immigrants are comfortable with their own established fellowship. Our biggest barrier is that culture is such an important part of the worshiping community and unless we can build a multicultural worshiping community it will be difficult to attract other ethnic groups.

CHAPTER - 3
Culture and Immigrants, Islamic Culture in North America and Culture and Communities

3.1 Culture and Immigrants

North America is a land of immigrants and almost all citizens of the world community can be found living here. These immigrant communities have many customs and values of their own. Recent history of North American immigrant communities reveals a growing significance of culture and its importance in religion. Culture barrier is a one of the major problems facing the North American churches. In the past, the American myth taught us that people come from different communities and different nations and become part of one nation and one community that is the United States of America. That myth is no longer true in terms of recent immigrants. **Many of the recent North American immigrants are church goers.**[1] Today, North American churches are divided according to their culture.

---

[1] K.P. Kuruvilla, *The Word Become Flesh* (Delhi: Cambridge Press, 2002), 13.

> So American Christianity has added to the usual expectations that the people who join our churches will become "like us." But with the rise of what Michael Novak called "the unmeltable ethnics," we observe people of many cultures and subcultures whose culture seems as "natural" to them as ours does to us, who like their art, music, style, and language (or dialect) about as much as we like ours, who are not motivated to "become circumcised" and become like us.[2]

To understand the religious life of new immigrants, we must also understand their culture, and the relationship of culture and religion in their home land.

The Asian American community in the United States is the fourth largest after whites, African American, and Latino/Latina.[3] Many of the Asian Christian immigrants are from Catholic or Anglican communions. There are Catholic and Anglican churches everywhere in North America, yet many of these immigrant communities have their own separate religious worship. It is their culture that separates them from the mainline North American churches. "The 'Asian American' identification with the community is both geographical and cultural (or spiritual, if you will). Little Tokyo, in Los Angeles: for instance, is to the residents both home and a cultural center, but to the Japanese Americans living outside of its boundary, it becomes: a cultural/spiritual Mecca."[4] Christian practices and faith are greatly influenced by the culture in which the church is situated. "Of these, life humanity, reason, society, and culture are not only powers but also values, goods to which

---

[2] Hunter, *Church for the Unchurched*, 62.

[3] Edmond Yee, *The Asian Americans Their History, Community, and Culture, Catching A Star: Transcultural Reflections on a Church for all People*, Richard J. Perry, Jr., Editor (Minneapolis, Minnesota: Lutheran University Press, 2004), 66. (Another title is listed in the bibliography, please check. Bibliography already changed please check for accuracy. OK)

[4] *Ibid.*, 67.

we have been attached by a necessary love."[5] As social beings we are closely attached to the society and culture that we know and claim. "Thus, for Indian immigrants, particularly non-Christians, religion has become the key symbol of identity and of difference from American society, and has come to represent their Indian heritage."[6]

Many of the migrants who settled in North America used to worship with their partner churches in North America. But gradually they left their partner churches and formed their own congregations to have fellowship with people of their own countries. These indigenous fellowships meet not only for worship but also to support each other. They help each other and understand their common needs and common problems. A cultural community also works for the betterment of its own people. Culture is an important part of peoples worship and fellowship. The common culture that they are a part of bonds them together in fellowship. North American immigrant communities may have the same faith and denomination as North American churches, but their culture is an important facet and gift in their worship and fellowship. They keep a close relationship with their partner churches, but remain as a separate group due to their common culture. "The point is that each denomination and each ethnic group within particular denominations can celebrate their distinctive traditions and still be renewed by the traditions of others and by the diversity in the New Testament."[7]

---

[5] Niebuhr, *Christ and Culture*, 250.

[6] Prema Kurien, *Gatherings in Diaspora: Religious Communities and the New Immigration: Becoming American by Becoming Hindu: Indian Americans Take Their Place at the Multicultural Table*, eds., R. Stephen Warner and Judith G. Wittner, (Philadelphia: Temple University Press, 1998), 45. (This entry is listed under Shoshanah Feher in the bibliography, please check, if same, shorten entry here. This is another article in the same book written Kurien. Please check the accuracy of the format. OK)

[7] David Rhoads, *The Challenge of Diversity* (Minneapolis: Augsburg Fortress, 1989), 27.

During the early seventies, Indian Christians started migrating to North America. They came for better economic prospects. Once they settled down as families in North America, religious worship became an important necessity in their lives. Many of these communities have partner churches in North America. First, they started worshiping with the North American partner churches. However, North American churches were alien to them in all respects: language, fellowship, and food. They were not the same for the immigrant community. So they formed their own congregations in North America. Often it was difficult for them to financially maintain a worshiping community. In spite of these difficulties, they found it necessary to create their own worshiping communities. They feel very much at home in their separate worship places. They worship in their native language. During fellowship time they talk in their own language, wear their national dress, enjoy their own food, and even share their common problems. As the first generation community, they often help each other in their needs. In every sense, these local worshiping communities were heaven for them in terms of comfort. Therefore, they started their own separate congregations in North America, not because of their faith, but because of cultural differences from their partner churches in North America.

The Syro-Malabar Catholic Church, a South Indian Catholic community is an immigrant community in North America. The Syro-Malabar and the Roman Catholics are two separate divisions of the Catholic Church in South India. The Syro-Malabar Christians claim that their ancestors from South India were converted by the apostle Saint Thomas, and the Roman Catholics believe to be the dissidents of the migrant churches from Rome.[8] They are divided in India, not because of their

---

[8] M. O. John, "The Malankara Orthodox Church Through the Centuries", *StGregorios Malankara Orthodox Syrian Church Silver Jubilee Souverir* (Oak Park, Illinois: St.Gregorios Orthodox Church, 2003), 141.

faith, but because of their tradition. For all practical purposes, the Syro-Malabar Church in North America is the same as the Catholic Church in North America. Their faith and hierarchy are the same as any Catholic diocese in the world except for their social and cultural differences. In 2001, Pope John Paul recognized the need for a separate diocese for the Syro-Malabar community, a South Indian Catholic church, which was under the Catholic diocese of North America. The main reason for this is that Christian churches have an important role in the day to day life of an immigrant community.

> Recognizing their suffering and their diversity, our simple suggestion, for the benefit of those who wish to provide social and/or spiritual care with the Asian Americans, is: the style, content, and delivery method of any social/spiritual care must take into account the national origin, the religio-cultural orientation and inclination, the perception of the world order, and the period of immigration of the specific group.[9]

Throughout the centuries people lived in the Diaspora looking for a better prospect outside of their homeland. They have also shown that culture was an important part, not only in their social life, but also in their religious life. "In the first century some five to six million Jews were living in Diaspora that is, more or less permanently settled outside Palestine."[10]

> The Diaspora had begun at least as early as the deportations of the Babylonian exiles, in the sixth century, and had been fed by subsequent dislocations through successive conquests of the homeland, but even more by voluntary

---

[9] Edmond Yee, *The Asian Americans Their History, Community, and Culture, Catching A Star*, 73. (Is this the same book/ author as listed in the bibliography? He has written only one article in this book. Please check the accuracy of the format both in footnote and bibliography. Thanks, OK)

[10] Wayne A. Meeks, *The First Urban Christians: The Social World of the Apostle Paul* (New Haven and London: Yale University Press, 2003), 34.

emigration in search of better economic opportunities than the limited space and wealth of Palestine could afford.[11]

They joined together to enjoy their common worship and fellowship, to enjoy their common history and culture, and to share their common problems. Jews in the Diaspora also joined together and continued their religious practices to enjoy their common history and culture.

> Like other immigrant groups in the cities, the Jews naturally joined together to continue familiar religious practices, to enjoy the society of relatives and others of common heritage, to settle internal disagreements, and to exert joint pressure to obtain rights and privileges from the larger community.[12]

History has taught us that immigrant communities always kept their culture and tradition as part of their lifestyle.

This phenomenon is true in every North American immigrant community. These communities often provide new immigrants with the comfort and security they need to survive in a new place unfamiliar to them. New immigrants keep their own culture and social behavior in these communities. Today there are many immigrant community churches in North America. African Americans, Chinese, Hispanics, Japanese, and Indian all are separate large communities in North America, and they all keep their separate history, culture, and heritage.

Culture and tradition are an important part of worship places and community. The reason for the separation of immigrants from North American churches was mainly due to their culture and tradition. "Our Church subculture has erected dozens of barriers that separate many people from the possibility of becoming disciples. Virtually all of these barriers

---

[11] *Ibid.*, 34.
[12] *Ibid.*, 34.

are essentially cultural barriers, and have little or nothing to do with "the faith once delivered to the saints."¹³

Culture and tradition have been a part of people's religious beliefs and practices and will always remain a part of their life and religion. **The history of Islamic religious life in North America is another example of the importance of culture and traditions in religious beliefs and practices.**

3.2 Islamic Culture in North America

The emergence of Islam in North America occurred during the later part of the nineteenth century: "Islam is a religion that has always been revitalized by migration. The waters of the faith, says one scholar, are so clear that they pick up the colors of the rocks they flow over."¹⁴ In the United States, roughly seven million people believe in and practice Islam. Islam is a foreign religion to Americans; however, in recent years it has become one of the fastest growing religions in America. In every major city in America, Islamic culture and influence are felt today. American Muslims have also grown in diversity in recent years: "For a long time Arabs, South Asians and African Americans were the dominant groups in the community. More recently, Hispanic and Caucasian Muslims combine with the children of immigrant Muslims to enhance the diversity of American Muslims."¹⁵ American Muslims represent people from all over the globe. "Today, the American Muslim community is comprised of people drawn from a wide-ranging ethnic and professional mix. Whether they are immigrants, indigenous American, or converts, all are united in the unique theistic experience that is Islam."¹⁶

---

¹³ Hunter, *Church for the Unchurched*, 64.

¹⁴ Eboo Patel, *Acts of Faith* (Massachusetts, Boston: Beacon Press, 2007), 176.

¹⁵ M.A. Muqtedar Khan, *American Muslims: Bridging Faith and Freedom* (Beltsville, Maryland: Amana Publications, 2002), 1.

¹⁶ Jane I. Smith, *Islam in America*, X.

Throughout Islamic history, congregations in Islamic tradition have appeared to serve multiple roles. **Islamic congregations have assumed** considerable significance for religious practice as well as their social context. In North America, Islam as a religion has its own distinctive cultural identity and values. Many of the Muslims in the Western world have already adopted the lifestyle of the Western society within the Islamic culture.

> But in the West, the combination of liberalism, democracy and respect for diversity in conjunction with prosperity, present a real challenge to Islam. If it can be demonstrated that Islam is not only relevant but also necessary for a good and virtuous life in spite of the attendance of democracy and freedom, then Islamic values will be truly globalized and Islam will not be in danger of becoming anachronistic.[17]

Thus, to a large extent, Muslims have overcome many of their disadvantages in religion, customs, and cultural differences in recent years. One of the significant events in the Islamic world during the last century was the Iranian Revolution of 1979. The Iranian Revolution and the after effects of the reign of Ayatollah Khomeini did not help the image of Islam in the Western world. Many of the things that Khomeini did to create an Islamic Republic in Iran were anti-western and gave a bad image to Islam in North America. The tragic events of 9/11 and the fear after was also a setback for Muslims' progress in North America. But, to some extent, 9/11 also helped the community to gain some influence and respect in North America. "In a rather curious way the tragic events of September 11 have also helped bring American Muslims into the mainstream of American life and increasingly the government and media are seeking their input."[18] Islamic history has shown us that in

---

[17] M.A. Muqtedar Khan, *American Muslims: Bridging Faith and Freedom*, 3.
[18] *Ibid.*, 2.

recent years it has emerged as a separate culture in North America. "The task of not only articulating but also manifesting a moderate, peaceful, tolerant, inclusive, compassionate and moral model of Islam falls on the American Muslim community."[19] One of the drawbacks of the Muslim community in North America was that the early North American Muslim immigrants tried to maintain a community of believers in a foreign context often without institutional support. **Los Angeles, New York, Chicago, Dearborn, and Boston** are some of the major cities where there are a large number of Muslim communities in North America. The major division in Islam between Shiite and Sunnis, and the ongoing fight between them also did not help to build up the image of Islam in North America.

American Muslims are at a crossroad today. American prosperity has attracted them here, but once they are here American policies in the Middle East have alienated them. In recent years, Islamic scholars have worked very hard to change the image of Muslims towards Americans and Americans towards Muslims. "Changes in American attitudes and policies toward Islam and Muslims will also be helpful in the transition to citizenship within the mind of each American Muslim."[20] The most important challenges Muslims in North America are facing today are not because of their culture or religion but because of the misunderstanding about their religion.

The life of Muslim women in the **twenty-first century** is a difficult one. Most often they are the victims of these changes and challenges, rather than beneficiaries.

> At times, they are victims of those who seek to protect them and at other times, those who seek to emancipate them,

---

[19] *Ibid.*, 3.
[20] *Ibid.*, 10.

oppress them. Even when it comes to historical processes, Muslim women are caught in the struggle between the imperialism of modernity and the intransigence of traditions.[21]

American Muslim women have an important role to play in uplifting the right of Muslim women worldwide. Muslim men worldwide enjoy an upper role in the society. Many verses in the Qur'an (2:228) allow equality between men and women. But traditionally, Islamic leaders have limited the scope of the Qur'an based on culture. Even in this century, in many places worldwide, Muslim women have been denied their right to education: "The only way the Muslim women's condition can be improved from within the Islamic tradition is if we have more women scholars of Islam, interpreting Islamic law and history with the explicit interest of emancipating women".[22] Traditionally, Muslim men have dominated the legal system in Islam. American women must take a leading role to fight for the freedom of Muslim women's rights to education, equality, and dignity.

American Muslim women are increasingly vocal in their insistence on equal rights and opportunities: "The fight for women's rights is perhaps more fierce in America than in the Muslim world because when Muslim American women participate in activities at the mosque they expect to be treated in the same way they are at their jobs and schools."[23] One of the most controversial matters in Western Islamic society is women's dress. In many matters in an Islamic community, including marriage, women do not have the freedom that men enjoy. Second generation Muslims in America are also facing

---

[21] *Ibid.*, 87.
[22] *Ibid.*, 93.
[23] Geneive Abdo, *Mecca and Main Street: Muslim Life in America After 9/11* (New York: Oxford University Press, 2006), 141.

many difficulties accommodating their religious customs and practices. Some of the main concerns that Muslims face in America are thus: the roles of women, the establishment and maintenance of a sound family structure suitable to the Western world, and provision for the needs of those who are reaching the end of their productive days. Contrary to their counterparts in the East, Muslim women are taking an active role in the Western society.

There is nothing in Islam to prohibit democracy and the democratic system of government. The fundamental principles of democracy — justice, freedom, fairness and equality — are also the principles of Islam. In many Muslim countries, democracy is the form of government. But many reject the form of democracy in the West because they do not agree with the policies of the West: "The large number of Muslims who came out to vote in the presidential elections in the US and those Muslims who vote in hundreds of millions in Pakistan, Bangladesh, Iran, Malaysia, Indonesia, Turkey, Egypt and elsewhere testify to their comfort with democracy."[24] Like in any other religion, Islam also upholds a form of theocracy.

The Muslim community in North America is well educated. American Muslims also encourage their children to get a good education. Many Muslim families often educate their children in their own families or separate Islamic schools in order to detach them from Western culture. Muslims living in America have numerous organizations for the guidance and support of the community. One of the primary tasks of these organizations is to identify and resolve prejudice against Muslim communities in North America. Many of these organizations are very helpful in resolving some of the problems facing Muslim communities.

---

[24] M.A. Muqtedar Khan, *American Muslims: Bridging Faith and Freedom*, 97.

Because Muslims in North America are a rapidly growing community, they **already have a felt presence** and started contributing to communities in many ways. Muslims have established many worship places in North America. In the past, Islamic culture and social values have contributed many valuable assets to the world community, and in the future North American society will also benefit from the teachings of the Islamic community: "The cultural tradition of contemporary Islam owes enormous debts to Indian architecture, Persian cuisine, Turkish poetry, Arabic calligraphy, and Greek philosophy. What colors will America add to Islam?"[25]

However, as a community, they are also facing many problems in North America. In order for Muslims to be a successful community in North America, they have to face some of these tough challenges: "The challenge for American Muslims is to educate our fellow non-Muslim citizens about us and to help Americans rise above the misinformation."[26]

The first generation of Muslim immigrants in North America is facing a very difficult problem today. There is a cultural gap between generations. This immigrant community in North America is trying to maintain two different cultures and two religious communities. The second generation immigrant community in North America is also facing many problems. The life of second generation immigrants in North America is very difficult and painful because they need to live in two worlds, that of their parents, and the other outside world, of which they are also a part.

---

[25] Eboo Patel, *Acts of Faith*, 176.
[26] Asma Gull Hasan, *American Muslims: The New Generation* (Lexington Avenue, New York: The Continuum International Publishing Group Inc, 2001), 11.

There is an identity crisis among young Muslims growing up in North America. At home, they need to observe and obey their parents' religion, culture, and other social habits, but outside, they have to be true Americans. If that young immigrant is a Muslim, the story is a much more difficult one to deal with. The problem lies not in Islamic faith or religion, but in the eyes of others who cannot tolerate their difference. If their religion is Islam, young people's life is much more difficult to cope with.

> Where are the Muslim leaders who understand this complex challenge, who are helping young people develop a coherent, relevant Muslim identity in the West? Most Muslim leaders are busy meeting other needs of the community-building mosques and Muslim councils, developing relationships with Western politicians and urban police departments. But most are not involved enough in the lives of young people.[27]

Social and political activists never address issues of spirituality and religion. Spirituality is one of the most essential tools for social harmony. Undoubtedly, the Islamic community in North America is forming a culture of its own in recent years.

Islam has a very rich tradition. Throughout world history, Islam has been at the center of many developments and major events. "For most of the history of Muslim cultures, tribalness has not been seen as something to be destroyed, but as an inherent tendency that must be informed by Divine principles of morality and an understanding of the House of Islam which must stand against unbelief."[28] The Muslim community has given many contributions to the world. There are many things that others can learn from the Muslim faith and religion. For example, every community has to learn something from the Muslim attitude toward prayer. For Muslims, prayer involves

---

[27] Eboo Patel, *Acts of Faith*, 13.
[28] Aminah Beverly McCloud, *African American Islam*, 164.

a total body response. It shows their spirituality and attitude of thanksgiving in their hearts. Prayer rituals are an important part of their community. No matter how busy they are, they will find time for prayer. They find a place for ritualized prayer, not only in homes and mosques, but wherever they are. Helping the poor and giving to the needy is another important requirement of Islamic religion. Fasting during the holy month of Ramadan is one more important duty required of Muslims. American Muslim communities also observe Ramadan and other duties observed by Islamic communities worldwide. During Ramadan, they give a good deal of attention to the importance of charitable outreach ministries. American Muslims also practice these rituals regularly. These rituals are very important for Muslims to worship God and to maintain their faith in God. American Muslims not able to practice these rituals regularly are also critical of some of these rituals.

American Muslims are facing a very difficult challenge these days to coexist with other cultures in North America. Western media has labeled them as hostile to the West due to the activities of Islamic fundamentalists all over the world. "Misunderstanding of Islam and the spreading of stereotypes about Muslims are as prevalent in U.S. society as the discrimination against overweight people and smokers."[29] Today, Jihad is a word misunderstood by non-Muslims: "Many non-Muslims are unaware of or misinformed about the true meaning of the term to begin with, and the current climate might cause them to assume that the word is synonymous with violence done by Muslims."[30] In recent years, especially after 9/11, the life of Muslims has been very difficult in America.

---

[29] Asma Gull Hasan, *American Muslim: The New Generation*, 11.
[30] John Kaltner, *Islam: What Non-Muslims Should Know* (Minneapolis: Augsburg Fortress Publishers, 2003), 130.

The Muslim community in North America is changing rapidly. According to Jane I. Smith, "American Islam changes each day as new people join the community."[31] While the majority of Muslims in America are African American and immigrants, a growing number of other Americans are choosing Islam as their religion. In general, American Islam is multiracial, multi-ethnic, and growing. Muslims among the African American population is a fast growing community. One of the reasons for the fast growth of Islam in the African American community is because of racial tensions. Many of their leaders have used religion to show their discomfort with the white American community.

3.3 Culture and Communities

The African American and Latino communities in North America are considerably large communities. In North America, they are concentrated in particular areas as communities. In their own particular communities, they maintain their own culture and identities. Their communities are very similar to the culture and traditions of their native land. They identify themselves in these communities as different from the North American mainland communities. It provides them with a cultural identity, unity, comfort, and the security they need to exist in a different culture. These communities often function like a country within a country. They have their own support systems, schools, and worship places. Their food, clothing, and language are similar to their native countries in these communities. They also share their common experience and their common problems in these communities. Black church, Hispanic church, and Asian church are all visible in these communities. Predominantly, in the

---

[31] Jane I. Smith, *Islam in America* (New York: Columbia University Press, 1999).

African American communities, black churches play a dominant role in fulfilling their cultural needs.

> Not only did it give birth to new institutions such as schools, banks, insurance companies, and low income housing, it also provided an academy and an arena for political activities, and it nurtured young talent for musical, dramatic, and artistic development.[32]

Their concentration in particular areas is not accidental. Besides racial tension and prejudice, culture also has an important role to play in their concentration.

This common identity can be seen everywhere in North America. North America is a land of immigrants, but the immigrant communities, whether they are African American, Hispanic, or Asian, have already established their presence as small communities in North America on the basis of their culture. Their small communities provide them with a sense of security and cultural freedom, which is very important for their existence.

The African American Muslim community in North America, also known as Black Muslims, is a fast growing community. Socially and politically, they have become one of the most powerful communities in recent years. They maintain a distinctive culture different from other communities. Their history can be traced to the dark days of slavery in North America.

> The dawn of twentieth-century America saw the land in a complex web of social relations between its black and white citizens. Blacks no longer had the protection of the federal government against discrimination and were forced to accept 'separate but equal' accommodations in education, hospitals, public toilets, restaurants, and so on.[33]

---

[32] C. Eric Lincoln & Lawrence H. Mamiya, *The Black Church in the African American Experience* (London: Duke University Press, 1990), 8.
[33] Aminah McCloud, *African American Islam*, 10.

In order to respond to various injustices against African Americans at every level of North American society, Black Muslims decided to stand together as a separate community within the United States. Along with it they sought a wider connection with Africans worldwide. Consequently, they decided to have spiritual ties with the worldwide Islamic communities. In 1913, Noble Drew Ali established the first known community in the eastern part of the United States with the help of Dr. Suliman. "To give some organizational structure to this growing system of communities, Ali set up the Moorish Divine and National Movement of North America, Inc., which served as an umbrella organization for fifteen temples." [34] Thus, the origin of the African American Islamic community is from these temple communities that were started to fight injustices against the African Americans.

One of the few successful African American Islamic communities in North America is the Nation of Islam community founded by Wali Fard Muhammad and developed by Elijah Muhammad. In its early years, they were very successful in attracting large numbers of followers. The core belief of this community was in Allah. "A fundamental belief in Allah as one with no sons or partners dominated the theology, with an ethical emphasis on man's ability to correct man." [35]

They have also adopted a way of belief in North America identical to the worldwide belief of Islamic communities. But in many respects, they were different from the mainstream Islamic communities worldwide. "Since the nation's agenda diverged somewhat from traditional Islamic doctrine, some 'orthodox' Muslims accused them of illicit innovation and,

---

[34] *Ibid.*, 11.
[35] *Ibid.*, 28.

indeed, heresy."³⁶ The main belief of the African American community was social justice. "For African Americans, the Qur'anic emphasis on social justice becomes, after tauheed, the highest priority."³⁷

There was considerable social and economic diversity within the African American Islamic community. Throughout history there have been tensions between the leaders regarding ideology and the way to achieve justice. Many even questioned the direction of Islam in North America and saw a need to reconnect it with the mainstream. Their political ideas were radical and received opposition from the mainstream American communities and even from within their own African American community. They maintain a separate culture of their own from the African American and worldwide Islamic communities.

> Their embrace of a universal Islamic worldview was not in immediate conflict with their need to confront America's racism and social injustice. On the contrary, whatever they knew about Islam, all seemed to know that it stood for social justice and personal responsibility.³⁸

Even though they had many problems, they were able to show an Islamic presence in North America. Due to the radical nature of Islamic extremism during the later part of the twentieth century, American Muslims repeatedly faced opposition and were called upon to explain their position and to denounce terrorist activities.

The African American Islamic community in many ways has helped to develop a sense of security and freedom for African Americans in North America. They must also be credited with many social and economic developments in the African American communities. They have been actively

---

³⁶ *Ibid.*, 32.
³⁷ *Ibid.*, 34.
³⁸ *Ibid.*, 38-39.

involved in social and political activities since the early part of the twentieth century. Their attempt was to establish separate communities within the United States and develop spiritual ties to the broader Islamic worldwide community. For that purpose, they established many places of worship in major cities in North America. These temple communities were helpful to the economically and socially disadvantaged African Americans. Many of the African American leaders used religion to show their discomfort with the white American community. "African-American Islamic expressions have maintained the Islamic notions of social justice, absolute faith in the one God, and willingness to assert Islam in the face of all odds-even against the American government and its armies."[39]

African American Islamic communities in North America are facing many challenges. The most important reason for their struggle is their distinctive culture. One of the major concerns of the African American Islamic communities in North America is the role of women in their communities. In every level of social life, Muslim women's freedom was limited when compared to men. Men have the freedom to choose to marry women from Christian and Jewish communities. Muslim women were allowed to marry only Muslim men. They have difficulty finding their partners. In direct conflict with the worldwide Islamic community, supervised dating before marriage was also allowed in the African American Islamic community. In every level of social life, African American Muslims find compromise between traditional Islamic practices and **Western culture** in North America. For example, polygamy was not allowed in these communities because of the law of the land. Divorce is discouraged, although permitted. Generally, when compared to global customs and practices of

---

[39] *Ibid.*, 166.

the Islamic community, African American Islamic social life is different and contained by Western law and culture.

Education of children is another main issue in the African American community. Absence of prayer in public schools and sex education are serious concerns for Muslim parents in North America. Islamic wealth problems also raise many questions in the Western economic system. **Zakat, to purify one's wealth by providing money to those in need is an important practice of Islam. Islam also prohibits accumulation of interest.** In general, the economic and social challenges of African American Muslims in North America are one of the major concerns. Political awareness in the community is very high due to the affiliation with the Islamic worldwide community. African American Islamic communities also participate in the war against Islamic countries. Their effort must be appreciated in terms of national pride and helping their country when it is in need. Most of their struggles in North America are due to the culture of Islamic community worldwide.

Another important challenge that the African American Islamic community in North America is facing today is economic. According to Islamic teachings everything that exists in the world is the property of Allah. All resources of this world are not the property of any individual but part of a common trust. The economic system in the West is in conflict with Islamic principles. "From an Islamic perspective, the fact that the profit is not the result of work is problematic." [40] The function of the banking system in the West is also questionable in Islamic teachings. Many in the African American community are economically poor. Unemployment is highest among the African American population. The African American Islamic community remained divided for most of the twentieth century.

---

[40] *Ibid.*, 133.

Some remain away from political activities and active in community work to uplift their economic conditions. **They have always supported African Americans for political office in spite of their religion.** In recent years they have made many political inroads. The recent success of Barack Obama in the United States presidential election is unparalleled in U.S. political history. "For African-Americans survival has meant group solidarity, with periodic alliances with powerful communities such as liberal white Christians and Jews."[41]

The African American Islamic community in North America is a fast growing community, keeping a tradition distinct from their counterparts. Often their interpretations are also misrepresented. They have already developed a separate culture of their own in North America. Western culture has had a big influence in their social and economic life in North America. Undoubtedly, African American Islam came to North America because of the social injustices suffered by the African American community. They had their struggles and setbacks, but they were also successful as a social group in their struggle for freedom in North America. Even in the first decade of the twentieth century, they were denied their right to vote. Islam helps the community to ensure their voice is heard and protects their right to life. In that regard, the African American Islamic community must have a prominent place in history.

The African American Islamic community in North America is diverse, but their common culture unites them. Their efforts to uplift the African American community in North America must be recognized. They were often disorganized, violent, and against established institutions, but their goal was the betterment of their society. "Having been deprived of the major aspects of culture, African-Africans struggled to establish

---

[41] *Ibid.*, 165.

themselves in all their diversity as a people, to fight racism and its violence, and to decide the nature of their relationship with their former legal masters."[42] Their main goal now is to uplift the community rather than follow the principles of their religion. In recent years, many have been working very hard behind the scenes to uplift the community as a mainstream Islamic community.

> Many are working hard to create a multicultural Islamic community, one that is color blind. They are inspiring African American youth to join their schools and organizations, breaking with their parents' tradition of praying, marrying, and associating only with Muslims from their same ethnic background.[43]

In spite of their problems, they are different from other communities, and their common culture binds them together.

---

[42] *Ibid.*, 167.
[43] Geneive Abdo, *Mecca and Main Street*, 9.

CHAPTER - 4
Indian Culture and Christianity in India

4.1 Indian Culture

India is a country of many religions and many cultures. Geographically, India is about one-third the size of the United States of America. However, India's population is about three times more than the United States. The Indian population, above 1 billion, is the second largest population in the world, after China. About one-fifth of the world population lives in India, whereas the size of India is only 2.4 percent of the world. More than two-thirds of the people are Hindus. Broadly speaking, Dravidians and Aryans constitute the Indian people. Besides these, there have been many groups, including Mongolians and Greeks **among Indian population**. There are many distinct cultural groups in India marked by differences in dress, food, social customs, beliefs, and practices. "The extraordinary size of India's population is matched by its diversity of races, religions, cultures, languages and customs."[1]

Hinduism, one of the major religions in India, is broad based in its faith and belief. Hinduism is neither a missionary nor a militant faith. One of the methods of prevention of conversion

---

[1] K.P. Kuruvilla, *The Word Become Flesh* (Delhi: Cambridge Press, 2002), 12.

in Hindu religion is social exclusion. Hinduism deeply entwines religious beliefs with social customs and practices, so that even when a person ceases to practice Hindu religion, he or she finds it difficult to break away from the social urges of his or her community. Another way of prevention is through absorption. Hindu religion, with its rich social and cultural values, can accommodate people of other religions. This is probably one of the main reasons why Buddhism, Jainism, and other religions that originated in India could not survive in India. Even Christianity, with a much different viewpoint than Hinduism, could not flourish in India. Every aspect of life of an individual of Christian faith can also be seen to parallel Hinduism. In Christianity, the cross provides the focus by which God and human suffering can be explained. Hinduism negates the reality of suffering, and Hindus consider it as *maya* or illusion. They also believe that the cycle of rebirth and suffering is removed once they attain *moksha* or salvation.

The basis for the geographic division of Indian states is mainly due to culture and language. Even within these states, we will see different languages and different cultures. One of the reasons for this division is related to the geographic nature of India. Without proper communication and exchange of culture between the hills and the valleys, communities developed their own cultures within their territories. They have their own customs, manners, culture, and their own religious beliefs. India as a whole is a religious community. About 95 percent of the Indian people are religious and worship some form of God.[2] Like food and clothing, religion is an essential part of Indian people's daily life. From birth to death, they depend on religion for everything. Regardless of religious affiliation, people also take part in all religious festivals. Religious harmony is one of the main reasons for the political existence of

---

[2] *Ibid.*, 13.

the country. "If there was ever a country which housed, so graphically and tensely, the 'many religious' and 'many poor,' it is India."[3]

Culture is a defining part of every Christian community in India. Baptism, confirmation, marriage, and burial are the important religious events in Indian Christian life. **According to many scholars Christian religion in India is more of a social institution than of practicing the teachings of Jesus Christ.** According to N.A. Palkiwala, one of the outstanding legal experts of post-independent India, said "Christianity has been tested and has failed in India, but the religion preached by Jesus Christ remains to be tried."[4] They also celebrate religious events as social events. The whole community takes part in religious events regardless of their belief or affiliation. Religious affiliation and acceptance are important for the social life of every family. In India, religions in many ways are prestige, power, and a way of existence. Acceptance in the community as a religious person is important for the life of every family in India. Indian society has an important role to play in all aspects of human life, and religion is also part of that whole picture. In this regard, religion has an important role in the community life in India. All religion in India is somewhat influenced by Hindu culture and traditions.

Expression of faith is an important element in Indian culture. According to P.D. Devanandan, a well known Indian theologian, every faith expresses itself in "cultus, creed and

---

[3] Paul F. Knitter, *One Earth Many Religions: Multi-faith Dialogue and Global Responsibility* (Maryknoll, New York: Orbis Books, 1995), 9.

[4] K.T. Thomas, "Christianity Remain Yet to be Practiced" *New Vision For a Changing World*, an Ecumenical Magazine, Pub. K.C.Mathew (Kottayam, India: Learners' Offset Press, Volume 4, no. 6, 2004): 9-11.

culture."⁵ Cultus includes liturgy, the sacramental rites, festivals, and other religious symbols and myths. Creed is faith in search of understanding, and culture is the value and social behavior expressing faith in human relations. From the point of view of the history of religion, it seems very clear that cultus precedes creed. Human response to the divine presence in the depth of the human spirit cannot be separated from its symbolic expressions. Christianity also must learn from the cultus and culture in order to be part of people's lives. Christianity in India learned many valuable lessons from the rich traditions of the Hindu culture. Indian Christianity is also very much indebted to the broader culture and traditions of the people of India.

All religions in India are somewhat indebted to Hindu culture and cultural practices. Hinduism has its own culture and tradition, and it has its own uniqueness as well. In India, culture prevails over the life experience of the people. In the midst of social injustice and economic suffering, Indians value their culture very dearly and maintain it with all effort.

Hinduism is a peace-loving religion. The influence of Hinduism can be found in all major religions of the world. Hinduism believes in the practice of nonviolence or *ahimsa*. Gandhiji, the father of the Indian nation, gives us a good example of ahimsa. According to him, all religions stood for truth and love. He interpreted the Indian concept of ahimsa as love in the Sermon on the Mount. Respect of the elderly is an important teaching in Hindu culture in India. According to Hindu practices, blessing comes not only from God, but also from the elderly. Century old practices of joint-family system, respect, protection, and care for the elderly are still part and parcel of the Indian family system. In recent times, the Indian legal system enacted laws to protect parents.

---

⁵ M.M. Thomas, *The Acknowledged Christ of the Indian Renaissance* (Madras: Christian Literature Society, 1970), 293.

Many centuries old traditional practices of Hindu culture are also part of every Christian church and Christian family. Christian churches in India are so much indebted to Hindu culture and traditions. Indian churches practice many Hindu customs and practices. Christian marriage ceremonies in India have so many similarities to Hindu marriages. Christian church festivals are also very similar to many Hindu temple festivals and celebrations. All religions in India are indebted to Hindu culture and its dominant traditions. "Tali," "sari," and other practices of Hindu weddings are part of every Christian marriage ceremony irrespective of denomination and faith. Even today, Christian churches follow many rituals of Indian culture. But Hindu religion also learned many lessons from the Christian culture. Christian missionaries were pioneers in starting educational institutions in India. Hindu religion also adopted the method of Christian gospel meetings and evangelization as part of their religious outreach in recent years.

Thus, Christianity in India inherited much from Hindu culture and traditions. And, the only group which can claim to represent a true Indian Christian culture is the Syrian Christians of Kerala. They have a deep rooted Christian faith and liturgical tradition, and social customs and cultural values very similar to Hindu customs. It is very important for a foreign religion to adapt the culture and social values of the country in order to survive. Christianity has elements of universality and can be neither Eastern nor Western. It is only by "Indianising" Christianity that we can hope to make India the home of Christ. "Indianisation means the understanding of the meaning of Christ for our situation and bringing the spiritual treasures of our nation to the feet of Christ." [6] It is the result

---

[6] Richard W. Taylor, *Society and Religion*, ed. M.M. Thomas (Madras: The Christian Institute for the Study of Religion and Society, 1976), 164.

of Indians experiencing Jesus Christ and finding their own channels of expression.

4.2 Christianity in India

The history of the origin of Christianity in India goes back to the earliest centuries. According to tradition, St. Thomas came to India to preach the gospel, converting high caste Hindu families and establishing churches along the south coastal regions in India.

> The earliest record about the apostolate of St. Thomas in India is the apocryphal work called the Acts of Judas Thomas, written in Syriac by the Edessa circle about the turn of the 3rd C.C.E. Besides this, a number of fragmentary passages in the writings of Origen, Eusebius of Caesarea, Refines of Aquilegia, Socrates, Ephraim of Nisei, Gregory Nazianzus, Ambrose, and Jerome speak in unambiguous terms about the Indian apostolate of St. Thomas.[7]

This tradition is supported by historical knowledge of trade routes between India and the Middle Eastern countries. Writings of the early Church Fathers also referred to the Apostolate of St. Thomas in India. The apocryphal book, *The Acts of Judas Thomas*, written in Edessa, Persia, around A.D. 180, contains many of the miraculous deeds performed by Thomas while preaching the gospel.[8] Tradition also records that John, Bishop of Persia and Great of India, signed the Acts of the Council of Nicea (A.D. 325).[9]

Christians of different denominations, traditions, and cultures live in India. The main concentration of the Christian

---

[7] Scott W. Sunquist, *A Dictionary of Asian Christianity* (Cambridge: Wm. B. Eerdmans, 2001), 366.
[8] John, *The Malankara Orthodox Church Through the Centuries*, 137.
[9] A.M Mundadan, *History of Christianity in India*, Vol. 1(Bangalore: Church History Association of India, 1984), 23.

population in India is along the coastal areas of the south and south west. St. Thomas Christian tradition teaches that their Christian tradition came from St. Thomas. One of the other notable Christian groups in India was led by Thomas of Cana in the fourth century. Tradition says that a group of about four hundred Persian Christians came to India under the leadership of Knai Thomas, a merchant from Cana, in AD 345.[10] The descendents of the Knai Thomas emigration continue to be known in Kerala today as the Knanaya Christians. Now they are a separate Christian community in India, and they have always kept a separate culture and tradition from other Christians in India.

European countries occupied India for many years. They established schools and educational facilities for local people. Their effort was to reform rural India through the means of education. European missionaries translated the Bible into local languages and made it available for the local people to read. It was very important for local people to understand the Bible in their own culture. Protestant missionaries brought much needed reform in India, and along with it they also brought more church divisions. St. Thomas Christians were split apart by the coming of Catholics and Protestants in India. "The ancient church of the Thomas Christians was left shattered into four major groups (Roman Syrian, Orthodox Syrian (Jacobite), Mar Thoma Syrian, and Anglican Syrian), not counting several smaller ones of which the Nestorian Syrians were the most noteworthy."[11]

The spread of Anglicanism in India created tension between the British and Thomas Christians. The main reason for the

---

[10] John, *The Malankara Orthodox Church Through the Centuries*, 137.

[11] Samuel Hugh Moffet, *A History of Christianity in Asia, Volume II: 1500-1900* (Maryknoll, New York: Orbis Books, 2005), 416.

tension was the importance of culture and traditions in the church. In the midst of this tension, the Anglican Bishop Wilson of Calcutta came up with certain programs of reformation in the church. As a result, in 1836, a church division occurred at the Mavelikara Synod, and that was the start of the Anglican Church in India. They kept the name and identified with Anglican churches in England in most respects. They also followed the practices and traditions of the Anglican churches, which were in many respects different from those of the Indian culture and tradition. In 1947, they joined the other Protestant churches in India and formed the Church of South India with a goal and view to evangelize the Indian sub-continent. The Church of South India is now the second largest Christian church in India, next only to the Catholic Church. They still closely follow Western culture and tradition in their worship.

Even after the separation of the Anglican churches, a large section of Syrian Christians continued their demand for reformation. The leader of this group was Abraham Malpan from Maramon, who revised the Syrian liturgy removing all prayers for the departed and invocation of saints from the order of worship. Under the leadership of Abraham Malpan, the Syrian group split again in 1837. They formed a new church with the idea of reform and without giving up the culture and tradition of the old church.

> Their great leader was a Jacobite priest, Abraham Malpan of Maramon (1796-1846), teacher of the Syriac Bible at the Syrian seminary in Kottayam, who stood firmly for the authority of Scripture over creeds, for translating the Bible and the liturgy from Syriac into the local language, Malayalam, and against processions for wooden images and prayers for the dead.[12]

---

[12] Moffet, *A History of Christianity in Asia*, 417.

The church now known as "Mar Thoma Church" is the result of that reform. Over the years, they have grown in Kerala, the southern most state of India, as one of the largest churches. Large numbers of Mar Thoma Christians now live in different parts of North America. History taught them the value and importance of culture and tradition in Christian fellowship and worship. In North America, they exist as a separate entity with close relationship with partner churches. Now they have strong leadership and a separate diocese in North America. They have flourished in recent years. They have also built many churches in different parts of North America.[13] They are reformers and very similar to the Anglicans in North America, but they are flourishing due to their distinct identity in worship and fellowship. They have a close relationship with the Episcopal Church in North America, but choose to remain separate with their own identity in order to keep their cultural distinctiveness and traditions. Today, they are an example of cultural identity to many Indian churches in North America. They originated in the name of reform, but they did not give up their identity and Indian culture. In North America, they followed their culture, and they are flourishing due to the lessons they learned from their historic beginning.

The origin of the Saint Thomas Evangelical Church of India in 1961 through a schism from the Mar Thoma Church was also for reform. The headquarters of this church is in Tiruvalla, very close to the headquarters of the Mar Thoma Church. The church also claims the ancestral history of the Mar Thoma Church. They wanted to be known as the reformed church in Kerala. They broke away from the church because they believed that the Mar Thoma Church had abandoned its fundamental

---

[13] T.M. Thomas and Mattackal Abraham, *In the Beginning: Formative Years of Mar Thoma Parishes in North America* (Tiruvalla, India: Christava Sahitya Samiti), 2008.

principles. While they stood for reform, they failed to realize the importance of culture in the worship place. They gave up many of the cultural practices continued by the Mar Thoma Church. They originated for reform, but they gave up the cultural identity and many of the Syrian rituals for the sake of reform. Their growth during the last fifty years is not what they had hoped for. In North America, they have many small congregations. They also have a structure and an organization in place for their growth in North America.

Before becoming independent in 1947, India was ruled by Britain. One of the benefits of European occupation in India was the expansion of the Christian religion. Many European countries established their own mission fields in India. Due to the culture and diverse geographical nature of India, Mission Societies were also established in many parts of India. The main aim of European mission work was to evangelize India, but rarely did they cooperate with each other in mission work. Anglicans, Methodists, and Presbyterians were all competing with each other for their existence.

> In 2000, there were 121 missions and evangelistic organizations in IMA's membership representing over 15,000 missionaries working in 1,400 locations in India and 10 other countries. Overall, India has over 22,000 missionaries, mostly working within India, but very much cross-culturally.[14]

One of the main reasons for the failure of mission coordination was also due to the diverse culture and geographical nature of India.

---

[14] (IMA) National federation for all Indian mission organizations working both within and outside India.

CHAPTER - 5
Church of South India (CSI) and Church of South India in North America

5.1 Church of South India (CSI)

The Church of South India was formed in 1947 by the union of the South India United Church, the Methodist Church in South India (British background), and the Anglican dioceses in the region. Union of the Church of South India was primarily based on the fact that the Church is a Body of Christ. According to J. E. Lesslie Newbigin:

> The Church is not primarily an association based on agreement about theological propositions. It is a unity of persons in the Body of Christ, represented locally by congregations in which Christ is present in the midst in Word and Sacrament, and through which He reaches out to save the world outside.[1]

The Church of South India is a united church in south India, and it is the second largest Christian denomination after the Catholic Church. It was the first merger to combine Episcopal, Presbyterian, and Congregational elements of polity in a single church order. "Looking at the history of the Church over the

---

[1] J. E. Lesslie Newbigin, *The Reunion of the Church* (London: SCM Press Ltd, 1960), 182.

centuries, this memorable event appeared little short of a miracle."² The Church of South India is the union of Episcopal and non Episcopal churches. The Church of South India was formed with a view to evangelize India. "The unique union of three great Churches - the South India United Church, the Methodists and the Anglicans – on September 27, 1947 was an adventure of faith."³

It came as a result of long negotiations between the Protestant churches in India. It took them almost twenty-eight years to reach an agreement.

> The formation of the CSI can be traced directly to the modern ecumenical movement and the International Missionary Conference in 1910 at Edinburgh. The recommendation for cooperation in mission among the churches led to joint evangelistic outreach by several churches in South India from 1918.⁴

In 1919, Protestant missionaries in India came together at Tranquebar with a view to co-ordinate their effort of mission work. V. S Azariah of the Anglican Church and Meshack Peter of the South India United Church were the organizers of the meeting under the sponsorship of the Evangelistic Forward Movement. Thirty-one Indians and two foreign missionaries met at Tranquebar in May 1919, to discuss church union. A manifesto proposing a union of their churches was adopted and was signed by seven Anglicans and twenty-six members of the South India United Church, including two non-Indians. This manifesto led to the beginning of negotiations that culminated in the formation of the Church of South India in 1947. After nine years of consultation the Scheme of Union was published in 1929 and some additions were made in the

---

² K. M. George, *Church of South India Life in Union (1947-1997)* (Kashmere Gate, Delhi: Cambridge Press, 1999), 1.
³ George, *Church of South India Life in Union (1947-1997)*, 1.
⁴ Scott W. Sunquist, *A Dictionary of Asian Christianity*, 175.

reprinting in 1944. The Anglicans were enabled to continue by the general, although cautious, approval of the Lambeth Conference in 1920 and 1930. Approval was voted by the Methodist Church in 1943, the Church of India in 1945, and the South India United Church in 1946. "The CSI is the first united church which brought together Episcopal and non-Episcopal churches into a new Episcopal church."[5] The major stumbling block in the negotiation was episcopacy.

> The Church of South India is the Church constituted by the union, in 1947, of the Madras, Madura, Malabar, Jaffna, Kannada, Telugu and Travancore Church Councils of the South India United Church; the South India Province of the Methodist church, comprising the Madras, Trichinopoly, Hyderabad and Mysore districts, and the dioceses of Madras, Dornakal, Tinnevelly, and Travancore and Cochin in the Church of India, Burma and Ceylon, in which in 1950 merged the North Tamil Church Council of the South India United Church, in 1958 the Bombay Karnataka Council of the United Basel Mission church in India, in 1968 the South Canara and Coorg District Council of the United Basel Mission church in India , and in 1975 the Anglican Congregations in the Nandyal Diocesan area.[6]

The Church was inaugurated at Madras on September 27, 1947. At the time of the union nine bishops were consecrated by the three Anglican bishops.

It was the conviction at the outset that the Church of South India must not rest content with being a united church, but should strive to be a uniting church, taking the lead in promoting a complete union of the Protestant and Orthodox Churches in South India. "The CSI did not imagine itself just another new Church, but hopes that it would serve as a catalyst

---

[5] *Ibid.*, 175.
[6] The Constitution of the Church of South India (Chennai, India: AVM Offset Printers, 2003), 3.

to bring together other Churches into wider union."[7] Conversations with Lutherans and two Conventions of Baptists began in 1948. The Baptists suspended negotiations the next year. The Lutheran and the Church of South India talks continued, and by 1966 they agreed in all matters of doctrine and had come to the consideration of episcopacy.

The formation of the Church of South India is a historical event. J. E. Lesslie Newbigin states that "the Church of South India is-of course-very far from being the only example of the reunion of churches in our time. There have been many others, and some very significant ones have taken place in the ten years since the C.S.I was inaugurated."[8] But it was the first time ever that such a unification happened. Newbigin highlights the unification of the CSI as follows:

> But it is generally conceded that there is as yet no other union of Churches quite comparable with that in South India in respect of the variety of traditions which it incorporates.[9]

Episcopal, Presbyterian, and congregational elements of the Christian churches came together for the first time as one church in the Church of South India.

> The Church of South India recognizes that Episcopal, presbyteral, and congregational elements must all have their place in its order of life, and that the episcopate, the presbyterate, and the congregation of the faithful should all in their several spheres have responsibility and exercise authority in the life and work of the Church, in its governance and administration, in its evangelistic and pastoral work, in its discipline, and in its worship.[10]

---

[7] George, *Church of South India Life in Union (1947-1997)*, 13.
[8] Newbigin, *The Reunion of the Church*, xiv.
[9] *Ibid.*, xiv.
[10] The Constitution of the Church of South India, 11.

The Church of South India is a united and unifying church, and the main mission of the church is to evangelize India where more than ninety-seven percent of the people are non-Christians. "The Church of South India is a united and uniting Church. The purpose of unity is that the Church might be more effective in its witness to the Gospel in India, as it is expressed in the prayer of Jesus Christ 'that they all (disciples) may be one that the world may believe that you have sent me' (John 17:21).[11]

It was agreed that all presbyters or ministers of the uniting churches would be accepted as equal, but that henceforth all ordinations would be done by bishops with presbyters assisting. It was expected that complete unification of the ministry would be effected in about thirty years. The Church of South India has a democratic constitution and is divided into twenty-two dioceses in four southern states of India. The dioceses are constituted according to geographical dimensions and are independent of each other in carrying out their ministry. The dioceses have autonomy within their own area, and the churches have great liberty in following their former traditions and ways of worship. The constitution lays much stress on the general ministry of the laity and the specific forms in which it can be performed. The pastoral, evangelistic, and teaching functions of the bishops are stressed even above liturgical, disciplinary, and administrative duties. The Order of the Holy Eucharist or The Lord's Supper bears evidence of the several traditions united in the church, but it transmits the essential elements from the early church, and it is influential in liturgical reforms abroad. According to Newbigin, "There is the closest possible connection between the acceptance of the missionary obligation and the acceptance of the obligation of

---

[11] The Constitution of the Church of South India, 25.

unity. That which makes the Church one is what makes it a mission to the world."[12]

The Synod is the supreme legislative body of the Church of South India. Laymen actually have greater numbers in the Synod than clergy. Synod meets once every two years and carries out all administrative matters. Synod officers are the Moderator, the Deputy Moderator, the General Secretary, and the Treasurer. They are elected for a term of two years. The Moderator and the Deputy Moderator are elected from among the diocesan bishops.

At the time of the unification, the consensus among the partner churches was not to form congregations outside the boundary of the Church of South India in India. The policy of the church was that when members go out of their territory they should worship with their partner churches. "Those members of the Church of South India living outside the above mentioned geographical area are encouraged to seek membership in churches which are in communion with the Church of South India." [13] There are many traditions in the Church of South India that are not originally from the Indian culture. In recent years, many of these rituals and traditions are changing or have changed. "The reason is that the Creeds, confessions and doctrinal statements of the organized, institutional churches are felt to be alien to the Indian religious and cultural traditions."[14] The vision of church leaders at the time of unification was not beyond South India. The leaders also failed to recognize the importance of culture in religious worship.

---

[12] Newbigin, *The Reunion of the Church*, 11.
[13] The Constitution of the Church of South India, 29.
[14] Kuruvilla, *The Word Become Flesh*, 3-4.

5.2 Church of South India in North America

South Indian CSI Christians started migrating to North America in large numbers during the later part of the 1970s. They came to North America in search of better prospects. According to the policies of the Church hierarchy, soon after they settled down, they started worshipping with their partner churches. One of the early problems they faced with their Church of South India partner churches was that those partners are not a united church in North America. The Church of South India partners in North America: Presbyterian, Methodist, Anglican, and the United Church of Christ — are not united and often they compete for denominational existence. There also exist many worship and theological differences between denominations. During the seventies, North America was not completely a just society. Language, color, race, and customs were all reasons for prejudice. Their language, custom, culture, and manners all were alien to these new immigrants. And often new immigrants from different cultures were not welcome in their fellowship. Very soon, the Church of South India new immigrant community found that they were not comfortable nor welcome in North American churches. Culture was an important reason for their discomfort.

In North America, the South Indian migrant community found it very hard to cope with the cultural practices of the partner churches within their church community. One of the reasons was social practices and language. Many elderly people found it very difficult to cope with the social practices **such as embracing by opposite sex during kiss of peace and teachings in favor of homosexual practices. Language also is a problem for many of the elderly.** Social practices in North American Western culture often clash with the Eastern values of family and sexuality. Faith expression in one's own native language also is an important aspect of a worshiping community. Language, dress, food, customs, manners, and sexual preference support needs, and in all matters of a church **community,** culture plays an important part. It became a struggle for the early Church of South India immigrants to worship with their partner churches in North America. Therefore, they formed their own fellowship to worship even without the approval of the Church of South India hierarchy in India. It was not an isolated event in the history of the churches.

These churches in many cases have similar faith and worship life, but the church culture remains the stumbling block separating them. The Eastern culture in which these immigrants grew up had little place in Western civilization. Western community and culture also did not always welcome these new immigrants. New immigrants found it entirely difficult to accept the cultural practices of Western countries in their worship places. It was very hard for the newcomers to abandon a culture they inherited from their forefathers and with which they were born and had practiced all their lives. It was unthinkable for the worshiping community also to accept a moral value which is opposite of their native culture. What they had learned and considered wrong in their lifetime now became acceptable and virtuous in the new North American culture. What they had prohibited as part of a Christian community now became part of their very own new community and new culture. In many places, they had no option other than to form their own worship community in North America.

It did not take long for the new immigrants to organize separate congregations during the early part of the 80s. One of the major problems they faced in the new community was the blessing of their church hierarchy in India. Initially, they formed ecumenical worship services with their fellow South Indian Christians in North America. The Church of South India members played a leading role in organizing and maintaining many of these early ecumenical fellowships. Power struggles and financial greed played a major role in the downfall of these ecumenical South Indian immigrant congregations. In many cases, denominations other than the Church of South India hierarchy gave permission to their members to form separate congregations. Hence, they were forced to start separate congregations in North America. Church of South India members were the last group to form such congregations. In many cases, they used the facilities of their partner churches. Of all the major denominations of the South Indian churches, only the Church of South India hierarchy did not help or cooperate with these emerging immigrant congregations.

Events during the last fifty years changed the concept of unification. The policy and guideline of the Church of South India Synod, not to form congregations outside its boundaries, does not sound right in this century because culture is an important part of a worshiping community. In recent years, large numbers of people traveled outside its boundaries. During the last three decades, large numbers of Church of South India members have also immigrated to North America. The history of the church during the last few decades proved that it is not a workable agreement anymore to restrict membership only to South India and encourage members to worship only with their partner churches. In many places, these new immigrants kept a close relationship with their partner churches. In some cases, they even used the facilities of their partners. It was not faith or beliefs that separated them, but it was culture that made a difference. All other South Indian hierarchy, except the Church of South India, had already realized that reality.

In recent years, the congregations of the Church of South India have established their presence in North America. Now they have their separate worship and identity. In 1994, these congregations formed a council and registered as a separate entity in North America with the cooperation of the church hierarchy back in South India.

> Since the mid 1960's, there has been a significant influx of Christians from South India to North America. Finding ourselves in the midst of great diversity on this continent due to differences in culture and language, we, the Christians who follow the traditions of the Church of South India felt the need to be culturally and religiously bound together by the liturgical and ecclesiastical practices of the Church of South India. We, therefore, seek a structure to promote a unified, orderly and uniform practice among the Church of South India Congregations in North America.[15]

Since 1996, the North American CSI Council has been invited to the Church of South India Synod, the highest body of the church. But for several years, leaders of the Church of South India refused to accept North American Council's identity or existence. In recent years, North American CSI congregations have struggled for their existence. In 2003, after a long-standing request and negotiations, the Church of South India amended the constitution in order to accommodate these North American congregations.

> However, if they desire to keep their identity and fellowship with the church of South India, they may continue their identity as members of the Church of South India by organizing themselves into congregations recognized as such by the CSI Synod Executive Committee/Working Committee.[16]

The main objective of the council was to provide a common forum for contact with between the Church of South India Synod, various churches of South India Dioceses, and partner churches in North America within their cultural unity. The leaders of the Church of South India congregations felt finally

---

[15] From the preamble section of the Constitution of the Council of Church of South India Congregations in North America, ratified on August 23-24, 1994, by the Church of South India Synod Working Committee, 1.

[16] The Constitution of the Church of South India, 29-30.

able to form a Diaspora diocese for themselves in North America. It was not faith or liturgy that mainly changed the guiding principles of unification, but it was culture guiding the faith of the community. The community identified themselves with the culture of their forefathers even though as Indian Americans they are in a new community and within a new culture.

The Church of South India Anglican **community** in North America has flourished in recent years in spite of their struggles. At present, they have over 50 congregations scattered all over North America. In many cities they have built their own congregations.[17] They continue to overcome many challenges and obstacles in order to keep their cultural identity. Always their culture binds them together in their new Christian community. Usually they travel many miles to share in fellowship. But these struggles are not an obstacle to their cultural unity and fellowship. After long negotiations with the Church of South India Synod in 2003, the church hierarchy realized that it is for their common benefit that these congregations should and must exist, and the constitution of the Church of South India was amended to accommodate them. "The Moderator of the Church of South India or Diocesan bishops appointed by him shall have Episcopal oversight of such congregations."[18] **But the Moderator of the Church of South India and the diocesan bishops in India has their own dioceses and responsibilities.**

Many Church of South India congregations are in existence today in North America, but exist without a proper structure or organization. They have no permanent hierarchy

---

[17] L. E. Sahanam, "Can we formulate a new ministerial policy?" *Church of South India 21st Annual Family and Youth Conference Souvenir*, July 2007, 36-42.
[18] The Constitution of the Church of South India, 30.

to resolve their problems or to guide them in North America. Pastoral care for these congregations is one of the major problems. They have no permanent arrangements for pastoral care. After years of struggle and many requests and meetings these congregations are still without proper leadership and guidance. They are yet to be recognized as an organized entity of the Church of South India. Church hierarchy still refuses to accept them and recognize them as separate entities with all the rights and responsibilities of a diocese or as a Diaspora diocese/community of their own. They still have no proper episcopal authority or structure. They also often experience intergenerational conflict. Without proper guidance and structure they may not exist forever.

The members of the Church of South India in North America are facing many problems. They are in many ways different from their counterparts in South India. They have an emerging culture that is not of India or North America. In recent years, they have formed a unique community of South Indian Christians in North America. They have adopted many things from the North American community. In many places, they have modified their worship liturgy to accommodate the needs of North American people. They speak English as well as Malayalam. Their worship is both in English and Malayalam. In many respects, they are also unique in history. They are forming a new culture in North America, which is different from their counterparts in India and their partner churches in North America. Their problems are also unique. They have no path to direct them. Every new day brings a new challenge for which they must find new answers. The younger generation is growing up in a culture different than their forefathers. For the first generation it is often hard to accept and cope with the struggles of the younger generations. They must cope with two different cultures. Many of their families, their dear ones, are in South India. In recent years, the Church of South India in North America has begun forming a new culture, a culture not of their forefathers or their new country, but a blended culture of their own. The younger generation is a new cultural generation in every respect. Culture and church also have an important role in the life of the younger generation. In current times, youth participation in churches and youth ministry in mainline churches is declining. The main reason is cultural. Traditional churches have failed to cope with the growing subculture of the young community in present times.

> The church, generally, has failed to adapt to the developing subculture of young people or to take seriously their concerns and causes. Furthermore, our teenagers and young adults are no more likely to adapt to churches perpetuating the 1950s than they are likely to buy their father's Oldsmobile.[19]

Traditional churches have ignored the value of culture across generations. The youth follow change, and traditional churches remain unchanged, resulting in the sharp divide and decline of the young population from the traditional churches. Cultural changes and church stagnation remain the stumbling block for uniting the young and old, cross-culturally.

One of the major problems facing members of the Church of South India community in North America is guidance from the hierarchy. In North America, Church of South India community has no proper guidance. They have no church constitution, historical precedence, or church leaders with a vision to guide them. They have no church hierarchy that understands the problems they are facing in North America. Today, they are facing an uphill battle, a battle for their existence, a battle to follow their ancestors' tradition, a battle for their faith, culture and religion. They have to deal with all

---

[19] Hunter, *Church for the Unchurched*, 63.

the problems in their new community themselves. They have to cope with their social, economic, and religious problems themselves. They have to deal with the problems of forming a new community, a new culture of their own in North America and their new society and new church. They also have to share in the troubles of their dear ones in their homeland in South India. Their problems are not simple for others to easily understand. Their problems are in many ways unique and complicated. Few outside their community understand their problems. Those who understand do not want to be involved, due to the complexity of the problems.

The refusal to allow the Church of South India members in North America to have their own diocese also hinders discipleship and growth of the church. Many members of the Church of South India have already left and joined organized worshiping communities of their fellow Christians in North America. Currently, the Church of South India in North America is at a crossroads, struggling to become a viable church, yet without any proper guidance or leadership. In recent years, struggles for power and financial greed have staggered the growth of the church, yet they remain together as a worshiping community, not mainly because of faith, but out of a deep need for cultural connection. These communities see hope in the church and the possibility of passing on their culture to the younger generation, but often they do not know how. They are more enthusiastic in their fellowship, again not so much because of their faith, but because of their tradition and culture. The Church of South India as a church community cannot exist long in North America without understanding the importance of their culture in faith and their fellowship.

The Marthoma Church, a reformed Church that broke away from the Eastern Church, realized the need and importance of culture in fellowship, so chose to reform their church within their culture. The history of the church shows that the main reason for the growth of the church was cultural. In North America, they understand the need of a separate culture for their church community. Today, they are a major community of South Indian people in many parts of North America. They have a structure and a strong diocesan leadership in North America.[20]

Tensions between cultures always existed in society. These tensions always existed and were part of every new community and civilization. It will remain for ever as long as religion and culture are in existence. Cultures, society, faith, and religion were connected and will remain connected for ever. Culture always played an important role in a worshiping community and will play the same role for ever.

---

[20] T.M. Thomas, *In the Beginning: Formative Years of Mar Thoma Parishes in North America* (Tiruvalla, India: Christava Sahitya Samiti, 2008).

Conclusion

Religion, culture, and faith are fully integrated. Culture is an integral part of fellowship, and fellowship is an important part of religious life. Religious practices and faith are very much influenced by the culture in which the religious fellowship is situated. From the first century forward, culture has played an important part in the fellowship of Christian churches. Historically, church and culture informed each other. The relationship of the church to its culture is evident in the history of religion universally. Human beings are social beings and are very much attached to their culture and civilization. "Of these, life, humanity, reason, society, and culture are not only powers but also values, goods to which we have been attached by a necessary love." [1]

In many respects, it is not faith that determines affiliation to the religious institution but culture. Culture and religion are closely connected. Culture strengthens religion, and religion influences culture. "It is easier, and perhaps more accurate, to suggest that when individuals and groups within our culture commit themselves to Christ they frequently (not always) use these and other features of our culture in a more Christian way than those who do not have such a Christian commitment."[2]

---

[1] Niebuhr, *Christ and Culture*, 250.
[2] Kraft, *Christianity in Culture*, 51.

Culture also unites people. "That which we call a rose By any other name would smell as sweet."[3] This quote has been one of the most famous lines of all times. In most languages, there is a word to define what we all see as a rose. When we see a rose, we all can agree that it is a rose, but if we all try to explain to one another what a rose is without seeing it, it would be difficult to understand what each of us is talking about. This is the common problem among different cultures. Each culture has a common way of defining things as they are, but when people try to translate from one culture to another, the thing often seems to get lost in translation. This is not only true in language but also true at every level of human behavior. Often we get lost in the cultural tradition. Many cultures express love not in words but in action. Only one's own culture will understand the language even though it is a common language. Culture has played a dominant role throughout the centuries. The fresh and diverse Christian culture served well the first-century Christians because it held them together when they were facing common problems in their community, so too today, culture has power to hold religious communities together.

In recent years as suburbs grew with immigrants, immigrant communities have shaped and founded their own churches even though they are partner churches with many North American mainline churches.

> When a church employs the language, music, style, architecture, art forms, and other forms of the target population's culture, Christianity then has a fair chance to become contagious within their ranks. But when the church's communication forms are alien to the host population, they may never perceive that Christianity's God is for people like them.[4]

---

[3] A quote from *Romeo & Juliet* by William Shakespeare.
[4] Hunter, *Church for the Unchurched*, 58.

Conclusion

This trend will continue as long the culture of the immigrant communities remains separate from the North American traditional churches.

> Regardless of what its theology eventually matures into, however, there is no question that the Great emergence is the configuration of Christianity which is in ascendancy. It is just as certain that both the Roman and the Protestant communion in North America will have to readjust themselves to accommodate the stresses of such massive changes in the culture and in the church.[5]

In the worshiping community, whether it is Christian, Hindu, Buddhist or Muslim, the role of culture will be central. We have seen during the course of this study that culture played a major role in every community, every society, and in all religions. Throughout the centuries communities were captives of their culture. We are captive of our culture. Every level of our life is controlled by our culture. It was true yesterday, is today, and it will be true for years to come. This was true in the first century Christian fellowship. It is also evident in the history of all South Indian churches, including the Mar Thoma Church, since its beginning in 1842, culture played a key role. The reason why Mar Thoma churches and Syro-Malabar churches are flourishing in North America is because they have always understood the value and importance of their forefather's culture in their worship places. Immigrant communities in North America are captives of their forefather's culture. The Church of South India communities of North America are not any different. The hierarchy of the Church of South India must also understand this important lesson. They must amend the constitution of the Church so that the new immigrant community in North America has equal rights and responsibilities as other dioceses in South India. The Church of South India may be the first united church in the world, but

---

[5] Tickle, *The Great Emergence*, 162.

the new culture they are forming in North American communities must celebrate and understand the value of their forefather's culture. The Church of South India must learn that important lesson and without it The Church of South India will not survive long in North America.

Bibliography

Abdo, Geneive. *Mecca and Main Street: Muslim Life in America After 9/11.* New York: Oxford University Press, 2006.

Azariah, V.S. *Christ in Indian Villages.* London: SCM Press, 1930.

Boyd, Robin. *An Introduction to Indian Christian Theology.* Delhi, India: ISPCK, 1969.

Brown, Terry ed. *Other Voices, Other Worlds.* New York: Church Publishing Incorporated, 2006.

Ehrman, Bart D. *The New Testament: A Historical Introduction to the Early Christian Writings.* New York: Oxford University Press, 2000.

Flanders, Henry Jackson, Robert Wilson Crapps, and David Anthony Smith. *People of the Covenant.* New York: Oxford University Press, Inc., 1996.

George, K. M. . *Church of South India Life in Union (1947-1997).* Delhi: Cambridge Press, 1999.

Haddad, Yvonne Yazbeck, ed. *The Muslims of America.* NewYork: Oxford University Press, 1991.

Harrelson, Walter. *The Ten Commandments and Human Rights.* Philadelphia: Fortress Press, 1980.

Hasan, Asma Gull. *American Muslims: The New Generation.* New York: The Continuum International Publishing Group Inc, 2001.

Hunter III, George G. *Church for the Unchurched: the rebirth of "apostolic congregations" across the American mission field.* Nashville, Tennessee: Abingdon Press, 1996.

John, M. O. "The Malankara Orthodox Church Through the Centuries" *St.* Gregorios Malankara Orthodox Syrian Church Silver Jubilee Souverir. Oak Park, Illinois 20003: 137-149.

Joly, Eugene. *What is Faith?*: Translated from the French by Dom Illtyd Trethowan. New York: Hawthorn Books Publishers, 1958.

Kaltner, John. *Islam: What Non-Muslims Should Know*. Minneapolis: Augsburg Fortress Publishers, 2003.

Khan, M.A. Muqtedar. *American Muslims: Bridging Faith and Freedom*. Beltsville, Maryland: Amana Publications, 2002.

Knitter, Paul F. *One Earth Many Religions: Multi-faith Dialogue and Global Responsibility*. Maryknoll, New York: Orbis Books, 1995.

Kraft, Charles H. *Christianity in Culture*. New York: Orbis Books, 1980.

Kroner, Richard. *Culture and Faith*. Chicago: The University of Chicago Press, 1951

Kuruvilla, K.P. *The Word Become Flesh: A Christological Paradigm for Doing Theology in India*. Delhi: Cambridge Press, 2002.

Legrand, Lucien. *The Bible on Culture*. Maryknoll, New York: Orbis Books, 2000.

Lincoln, C. Eric, and Lawrence H. Mamiya. *The Black Church in the African American Experience*. London: Duke University Press, 1990.

McCloud, Aminah Beverly. *African American Islam*. New York: Routledge, 1995.

Meeks, Wayne A. *The First Urban Christians: The Social World of the Apostle Paul*. New Haven and London: Yale University Press, 2003.

Moffet, Samuel Hugh. *A History of Christianity in Asia, Volume II: 1500-1900*. Maryknoll, New York: Orbis Books, 2005.

Mundadan, A.M. *History of Christianity in India*, Vol. 1. Bangalore: Church History Association of India, 1984.

Newbigin, J.E. Lesslie. *The Reunion of the Church*. London: SCM Press Ltd, 1960.

Niebuhr, H. Richard. *Christ and Culture*. New York: Harper & Row Publishers, 1975.

Nirmal, A.P. *Towards a Christian Dalit Theology in Frontiers in Asian Christian Theology*. Edited by R.S.Sugirtharaja. Maryknoll, New York: Orbis Books, 1994.

Osiek, Carolyn, and Margaret Y. Macdonald with Janet H. Tulloch. *A Woman's Place: House Churches in Earliest Christianity*. Minneapolis: Fortress Press, 2006.

Patel, Eboo. *Acts of Faith*. Boston: Beacon Press, 2007.

Patrick, Dale. *Old Testament Law*. Louisville, Kentucky: John Knox Press, 1985.

Perry Jr., Richard J. *Catching A Star: Transcultural Reflections on a Church for All People*.Minneapolis, Minnesota: Lutheran University Press, 2004.

Bibliography

Rajamanickam S., S.J. "Roberto de Nobili, and Adaptation." *Indian Church History Review*1 (Nov. 2, 1967): 83-91. page numbers.

Rhoads, David. *The Challenge of Diversity*. Minneapolis: Augsburg Fortress, 1989.

Ruether, Rosemary Radford. *Sexism and God-Talk*. Boston: Beacon Press Books, 1993.

Sahanam, L.E. "Can We Formulate a New Ministerial Policy" *Church of South India 21st Annual Family and Youth Conference Souvenir*, (July 2007): 36-42.

Shorter, Aylward. *Toward a Theology of Inculturation*. London: Biddles Ltd, 1988.

Smith, Jane I. *Islam in America*. New York: Columbia University Press, 1999.

Stassen, Glen H., D.M. Yeager, and John Howard Yoder. *Authentic Transformation*. Nashville: Abingdon Press, 1996.

Sugirtharajah, R. S. Edited *Voices From the Margins: Interpreting the Bible in the Third World*. Maryknoll, New York: Orbis Books, 1995.

Sunquist, Scott W. *A Dictionary of Asian Christianity*. Cambridge: Wm. B. Eerdmans Publishing Company, 2001.

Taylor, Richard W. *Society and Religion*. Ed. M.M. Thomas, Madras: The Christian Institute for the Study of Religion and Society, 1976.

The Church of South India in North America. "The Constitution of the Council of Church of South India Congregations in North America," ratified by the Church of South India Synod Working Committee on August 23-24, 1994.

The Church of South India. *The Constitution of the Church of South India*. Chennai: AVM Offset Printers, 2003.

Mathew K.C. "Christianity Remain Yet to be Practiced" *New Vision For a Changing World*, an Ecumenical Magazine. Kottayam, India, Volume 4, no. 6, (2004): 9-11.

Thomas, M.M. *The Acknowledged Christ of the Indian Renaissance*. Madras: Christian Literature Society, 1970.

Thomas, M.M. *Society and Religion*. Edited by Richard W. Taylor. Madras: Christian Literature Society, 1976.

Thomas, T.M., and Mattackal Abraham. *In the Beginning: Formative Years of Mar Thoma Parishes in North America*. Tiruvalla, India: Christava Sahitya Samiti, 2008.

Tickle, Phyllis. *The Great Emergence: How Christianity is Changing and Why*. Grand Rapids, Michigan: Baker Books, 2008.

Tillich, Paul. *Theology of Culture*. New York: Oxford University Press, 1959.

Vallet, Ronald E. *The Steward Living in Covenant: A New Perspective on Old Testament Stories*. Grand Rapids, Michigan: Wm. B. Eerdmans Publishing Company, 2001.

Warner, Stephen, and Judith G. Wittner, eds., *Gatherings in Diaspora: Religious Communities and the New Immigration*. Philadelphia: Temple University Press, 1998.

www.ingramcontent.com/pod-product-compliance
Lightning Source LLC
Chambersburg PA
CBHW032128090426
42743CB00007B/512